The Individuals with Disabilities Education Act as Amended in 2004

Second Edition

Rud Turnbull
The Beach Center on Disability
University of Kansas

Nancy Huerta

Matthew Stowe

with special assistance by **Louis Weldon** and **Suzanne Schrandt**

Boston, Massachusetts
Columbus, Ohio

Between the time website information is gathered and then published, it is not unusual for some sites to have closed. Also, the transcription of URLs can result in typographical errors. The publisher would appreciate notification where these errors occur so that they may be corrected in subsequent editions.

This book was printed and bound by R.R. Donnelley & Sons Company. The cover was printed by Phoenix Color Corp.

10 9 8 7 6 5 4 3 2 1
ISBN-13: 978-0-13-714911-7
ISBN-10:   0-13-714911-5

Table of Contents

Non-Discriminatory Evaluation: The Second of the Six Principles   **28**

Appropriate Education: The Third of the Six Principles   **40**

Overview

I. IDEA: A Brief History and Our Approach

Congress first enacted the Individuals with Disabilities Education Act in 1975 as P.L. 94-142, Education for All Handicapped Children Act. Since then, Congress has amended the law on several occasions, most recently in 2004 as P.L. 108-446, "Individuals with Disabilities Education Improvement Act."

For simplicity's sake, we refer to the 2004 law simply as "IDEA." That also is the "short title" that Congress gave it. Section 1400(a).

In this booklet, we describe the 2004 amendments that are most relevant to the education of students with disabilities and the significance of those amendments. We urge you to read the statute itself because we only digest it here.

Please note that we use the "1400" section designations because the 2004 amendments will be codified in 20 United States Code beginning at Section 1400. In doing this, we assume that the codification of the 2004 amendments will mirror the codification of the pre-2004 IDEA.

The basic organization of IDEA remains unchanged. IDEA consists of four parts or subdivisions. Part A declares the barriers, solutions, and national policy for educating students with disabilities. Part B authorizes funds to educate students ages 3-21. Under Part B, students receive a free appropriate public education (FAPE). Part C authorizes funds to educate infants and toddlers, ages birth/0 to 3. Part D authorizes national research, training, demonstration, and technical assistance activities. We discuss only Parts A, B, and C.

Please also note that the 2004 amendments raise questions that the U.S. Department of Education regulations may answer.

Where the U.S. Supreme Court cases interpreting the IDEA before Congress amended it in 2004 apparently still apply, we cite and briefly discuss them.

1

Because the 2004 law relates to other education and disability laws, we also discuss how it relates to them. We begin by describing IDEA's relationship to the federal education law that has the greatest effect on all students in all public schools, the No Child Left Behind Act, and to the two federal laws that prohibit discrimination against students with disabilities, Section 504 of the Rehabilitation Act and the Americans with Disabilities Act.

Next, we describe IDEA, starting with a general description and then digesting its provisions according to IDEA's six principles (Turnbull, Turnbull, Stowe, & Wilcox (2000), *Free Appropriate Public Education* (6th ed.). Denver: Love Publishing Co.).

II. IDEA (As Amended in 2004) and Its Relationship to the No Child Left Behind Act

Congress enacted the No Child Left Behind Act (NCLB) in 2001, and the President signed it in 2002, for the purpose of improving the education of all students, including those with disabilities, in all public schools in our country. NCLB rests on six major principles, and IDEA as amended aligns itself with NCLB. (When IDEA refers to NCLB, it refers to the Elementary and Secondary Education Act of 1965, because NCLB amends that law; ESEA is the principal law and NCLB amends it.)

The principle of accountability is that schools should educate all students in elementary and middle schools well enough that all of them will demonstrate proficiency in certain core academic subjects (English, mathematics, and others). The technique for achieving this principle is the standardized state or local assessments of student academic proficiency. IDEA provides that students with disabilities will participate in these assessments.

The principle of highly qualified teachers is that the teachers, themselves, must be proficient to teach and thus must meet certain federal and state standards before they are certified to teach. IDEA requires comparable standards for those who teach students with disabilities.

The principle of scientifically based intervention (also known as evidence-based intervention) is that highly qualified teachers will use research-based curricula and instructional methods. IDEA requires educators to use scientifically based methods in evaluating a student and then providing an appropriate education to the student.

The principle of local flexibility is that state and local educational agencies must have some discretion about how to use federal and state matching monies to secure the NCLB outcomes. IDEA grants some discretion to those agencies about how they use the IDEA funds.

The principle of safe schools is that effective teaching and learning can occur only in safe schools. IDEA sets out procedures and standards for disciplining students with disabilities.

The principle of parent participation and choice is that the parents of all students should have the opportunity to participate in their children's education and to remove their children from unsafe or failing schools. IDEA grants rights and private-school opportunities for students with disabilities.

III. IDEA and Its Relationship to Civil Rights Laws– Section 504 of the Rehabilitation Act and the Americans with Disabilities Act

Both NCLB and IDEA are education laws in that they authorize the federal government to provide funds to state and local educational agencies; they are grant-in-aid laws. The agencies must use the federal funds according to the principles and provisions of each law. Thus, IDEA is not only a grant-in-aid law, but also is a statute that creates procedures and standards that the agencies must follow and that the students have rights to receive and enforce.

Two other laws, however, are civil rights laws: Section 504 of the Rehabilitation Act Amendments (enacted in 1973) and the Americans with Disabilities Act (enacted in 1990). They differ from IDEA in several respects.

First, these laws prohibit discrimination in education against students with disabilities. To carry out their anti-discrimination, civil rights purposes, they create two related rights for students with disabilities: the right not to be subjected to discrimination based solely on their disabilities, and the right to reasonable accommodations in education.

Second, these laws do not authorize federal funds to be used by state and local educational agencies to educate students with disabilities. They are not grants-in-aid statutes, as NCLB and IDEA are.

Finally, a student with a disability may not qualify under IDEA as a child with a disability because, in spite of having a disability, the student does not need special education. Instead, the student needs reasonable accommodations in general (regular) education and nothing more. Section 504 and ADA provide that the student will receive those accommodations, but will not be classified as eligible under IDEA. There are fewer IDEA eligible students than Section 504/ADA protected students.

IV. IDEA and Its Six Principles

The IDEA has six principles, just as NCLB has its own six principles. These six principles constitute a seamless framework for understanding IDEA. The first four principles reflect the actual processes that schools follow in order to confer the benefits of a free appropriate education in the least restrictive environment for each student with a disability. The last two are the procedures that parents and students use to hold the schools accountable for carrying out the first four principles and to be partners with educators. Later in this booklet, we will describe each principle and all IDEA provisions that implement each principle. For now, however, it is sufficient to define each in the briefest of terms.

Zero reject reflects the process of enrollment and provides that every child with a disability (under IDEA) is entitled to a free appropriate public education.

Non-discriminatory evaluation occurs after the student enters school and when the school or others believe the student may have a disability and thus be entitled to IDEA's benefits.

Appropriate education occurs when the student receives individualized programs that benefit him or her in progressing toward the national policy goals.

Least restrictive environment reflects the presumption that the student's education will take place in a typical setting and with non-disabled students.

Procedural due process is a way for parents to hold schools accountable for that education and for schools to hold parents accountable for their child.

Parent participation ensures that parents and the student can be partners with educators in having a say about the student's education.

V. National Policy and IDEA, Section 1400(c)(1)

We have said that IDEA relates to NCLB, Section 504, and ADA, and we succinctly related it to those laws. Thus, IDEA aligns with general education and disability civil rights laws. More than that, however, IDEA reiterates America's policy related to people with disabilities.

> "Disability is a natural part of the human experience and in no way diminishes the right of individuals to participate in or contribute to society. Improving educational results for children with disabilities is an essential element of our national policy of ensuring equality of opportunity, full participation, independent living, and economic self-sufficiency for individuals with disabilities." Section 1400(c)(1).

◆ *Significance of Four Policy Goals*

Here, Congress sets out four national policy goals: equal opportunity, full participation, independent living, and economic self-sufficiency. IDEA and special education are the means for ensuring that students with disabilities will be educated to achieve these goals. Indeed, the desired outcomes of special education under IDEA and of reasonable accommodations under Section 504 and ADA are that students with disabilities will benefit from their education. The result of that benefit is that students with disabilities will be equally educated (with students who do not have disabilities) and become sufficiently prepared to participate fully in communities of their own choice, live as independently as they can, and be as able to work as possible.

VI. Nature of IDEA: Grant-in-Aid, Sections 1411, 1412, and 1413

As we noted above, IDEA authorizes federal funds to assist and induce state education agencies (SEAs) and local education agencies (LEAs) to carry out the Act's purposes and achieve the four national policy goals.

SEAs are eligible under Section 1412. Any state wanting federal aid under IDEA must apply for federal funding to the U.S. Secretary of Education. Eligibility is based on a showing that the state can meet all the provisions specifically set out by the law under Section 1412. If the state meets all the provisions, federal funding will be allotted to it.

LEAs are eligible under Section 1413. To receive federal funding that is "passed through" the SEA to the LEA, the LEA must file an application with the SEA, once every three years. The filing must include a showing that the LEA can and will comply with the specific guidelines set out in Section 1413.

◆ *Significance of the Conditions*
These provisions are the classic "carrot and stick" approach in federal grants-in-aid: the carrot is the receipt of federal funds and the stick is that the SEAs and LEAs must comply with IDEA. An SEA may choose not to receive IDEA funds (but none has done so) and thus avoid having to comply with the statute.

◆ *Significance of Granting Rights but Not Creating Entitlements*
Because IDEA is a grant-in-aid, it confers rights. But IDEA does not create a personal entitlement to special education. By contrast, the Social Security Act creates a personal entitlement to certain benefits if a person has retired or has a disability.

◆ *Significance for Anti-Discrimination Laws*
Section 504 and ADA supplement students' IDEA rights. A student may be entitled to benefits under both IDEA and 504/ADA. As we noted above, however, some students with impairments will not be eligible for IDEA but will still be protected by Section 504 and ADA.

VII. Major Purposes of IDEA, Section 1400(c)(4) and (5), and Section 1400(d)

Busting Barriers: IDEA identifies two barriers that have prevented children with disabilities from being educated effectively. These barriers have existed in spite of the fact that IDEA was first enacted in 1975. Accordingly, Section 1400(c)(4) provides that "[T]he implementation of this title has been impeded by low expectations, and an insufficient focus on applying replicable research on proven methods of teaching and learning for children with disabilities."

Offering Solutions: Section 1400(c)(5) identifies eight solutions to these barriers and, by its specific provisions, attempts to put them into place. The solutions are as follows:

"Almost 30 years of research and experience has demonstrated that the education of children with disabilities can be made more effective by–

1. "having high expectations for such children and ensuring their access to the general education curriculum in the regular classroom, to the maximum extent possible, in order to–

    a. "meet developmental goals and, to the maximum extent possible, the challenging expectations that have been established for all children; and

    b. "be prepared to lead productive and independent adult lives, to the maximum extent possible;

2. "strengthening the role and responsibility of parents and ensuring that families of such children have meaningful opportunities to participate in the education of their children at school and at home;

3. "coordinating this title with other local, educational service agency, State, and Federal school improvement efforts, including improvement efforts under the Elementary and Secondary Education Act of 1965, in order to ensure that such children benefit from such efforts and that special education can become a service for such children rather than a place where such children are sent;

4. "providing appropriate special education and related services, and aids and supports in the regular classroom, to such children, whenever appropriate;

5. "supporting high-quality, intensive preservice preparation and professional development for all personnel who work with children with disabilities in order to ensure that such personnel have the skills and knowledge necessary to improve the academic achievement and functional performance of children with disabilities, including the use of scientifically based instructional practices, to the maximum extent possible;

6. "providing incentives for whole-school approaches, scientifically based early reading programs, positive behavioral interventions and supports, and early intervening services to reduce the need to label children as disabled in order to address the learning and behavioral needs of such children;

7. "focusing resources on teaching and learning while reducing paperwork and requirements that do not assist in improving educational results; and

8. "supporting the development and use of technology, including assistive technology devices and assistive technology services, to maximize accessibility for children with disabilities."

◆ *Significance of the Eight Solutions*
The first solution relates to NCLB: having high and challenging expectations for all students, including those with disabilities; educating students with disabilities in the general curriculum; and assessing them for their proficiency to its curriculum. Doing all that will enable these students to be effective adults who will achieve the four national-policy outcomes. The second aligns with the

NCLB principle of parent participation and is implemented by the IDEA principle of parent participation. The third specifically and generally aligns IDEA with NCLB and makes clear that special education is the placement that occurs only after a general education placement is demonstrably inappropriate for the student. The fourth relates to the IDEA principles of appropriate education and least restrictive environment. The fifth mirrors the NCLB principle of highly qualified teachers and focuses on developing the capacities of schools to be effective in educating students with disabilities. The sixth also reflects NCLB by assuring that the interventions for students with disabilities will be carried out by all educators; it also reflects the NCLB principle of evidence-based interventions such as reading, positive behavioral interventions, and early intervention. The seventh addresses the complaint that there is too much focus on procedures and too little on outcomes by reducing paperwork and other non-educational requirements. The last refers to the Technology Assistance for Individuals with Disabilities Act (the "Tech Act") and is found in the "related services" provisions in IDEA.

Implementing National Policy Goals, Section 1400(d)(1) and (2): In order to carry out the four national policy goals, IDEA announces its discrete purposes:

1. "to ensure that all children with disabilities have available to them a free appropriate public education that emphasizes special education and related services designed to meet their unique needs and prepare them for further education, employment, and independent living;

2. "to ensure that the rights of children with disabilities and parents of such children are protected; and

3. "to assist States, localities, educational service agencies, and Federal agencies to provide for the education of all children with disabilities;

4. "to assist States in the implementation of a statewide, comprehensive, coordinated, multidisciplinary, interagency system of early intervention services for infants and toddlers with disabilities and their families;

5. "to ensure that educators and parents have the necessary tools to improve educational results for children with disabilities by supporting system improvement activities;

coordinated research and personnel preparation; coordinated technical assistance, dissemination, and support; and technology development and media services; and

6. "to assess, and ensure the effectiveness of, efforts to educate children with disabilities."

◆ **Significance of the Six Purposes**
The first purpose links special education to the four national policy outcomes. The second affirms that IDEA grants rights that, when implemented in schools, will lead to the outcomes. Thus, education should lead to designated adult-life outcomes. The third through sixth develop the capacity of SEAs and LEAs, and parents, to educate students so that the national goals will be achieved.

VIII. Definitions, Section 1401

IDEA defines its key terms alphabetically. We set out the definitions of IDEA's most frequently used terms, and we include new, significant definitions that align IDEA with NCLB and other laws.

"Assistive technology device": Includes virtually any item, regardless of its origin, that is used to "increase, maintain, or improve functional capacities of a child with a disability," but excludes "a medical device that is surgically implanted, or the replacement of such a device."

◆ **Significance**
The exclusion of a surgically implanted medical device clarifies that an SEA or LEA is not obligated to pay for or maintain devices such as cochlear implants. Otherwise, this is the same definition used in the Tech Act and in Section 504 of the Rehabilitation Act.

"Child with a disability" refers to a child

1. "with mental retardation, hearing impairments (including deafness), speech or language impairments, visual impairments (including blindness), serious emotional disturbance (hereinafter referred to in this title as

'emotional disturbance'), orthopedic impairments, autism, traumatic brain injury, other health impairments, or specific learning disabilities; and

2. "who, by reason thereof, needs special education and related services."

◆ *Significance*
There is no change from the prior law. This definition combines the "categorical" approach (listing the various categories of disabilities) with the "functional approach" (insisting that the disability cause the student to function in a way that requires special education intervention).

"Core Academic Subjects": These are the same as identified and defined in NCLB.

"Early Childhood Education and Children Ages 3 through 9": The term "child with a disability" for a child ages 3 through 9 (or any subset of that age range, including ages 3 through 5), may, at the discretion of the state and the local educational agency, include a child

1. "experiencing developmental delays, as defined by the State and as measured by appropriate diagnostic instruments and procedures, in one or more of the following areas: physical development, cognitive development, communication development, social or emotional development, or adaptive development; and

2. "who, by reason thereof, needs special education and related services."

◆ *Significance*
This provision allows, but does not require, a state to serve "at risk" students of designated ages. These students have not yet been identified as having a disability and needing special education; they are not yet "classified" or "made eligible" for special education. Nonetheless, because they are at risk for being classified into special education, the state may serve them in an effort to prevent them from being classified into special education. This is a way of preventing special education placement. It also expands the scope and coverage of IDEA to cover "at risk" students.

"Free appropriate public education" means special education and related services that–

1. "have been provided at public expense, under public supervision and direction, and without charge;

2. "meet the standards of the State educational agency;

3. "include an appropriate preschool, elementary school, or secondary school education in the State involved; and

4. "are provided in conformity with the individualized education program required under Section 1414(d)."

◆ *Significance*
No change from prior law.

"Highly Qualified" refers to the qualifications of special education teachers. As a general rule, the definition aligns IDEA with NCLB. There are, however, specific meanings of "highly qualified" for special education teachers as a whole profession, for those who teach to the alternative achievement standards, and for those who teach multiple subjects.

◆ *Significance*
The requirement for teachers to be highly qualified does not create a right of action on behalf of a student or class of students against an SEA or LEA that fails to employ a "highly qualified" teacher in special education, or, presumably, to compel a particular SEA or LEA employee to be highly qualified.

"Homeless children" has the meaning given the term under the McKinney-Vento Homeless Assistance Act (42.U.S.C. 11434(a)(2).

◆ *Significance*
The 2004 amendments add accountability for schools to find and serve homeless children within the district. This expansion of services shows a heightened awareness and responsibility on the effects of poverty on children and education.

"Limited English Proficient" is defined according to NCLB.

"Parent" includes a natural, adoptive, or foster parent, a legal guardian, an individual acting in the place of a natural or adoptive parent (including a grandparent, stepparent, or other relative) with whom the child lives, or an individual assigned to be a surrogate parent.

◆ *Significance*

This definition mirrors the changing demographics of American families, recognizes that various people function as "parents", and expands the range of individuals who are both responsible and accountable under IDEA.

"Related services" means "transportation, and such developmental, corrective, and other supportive services (including speech-language pathology and audiology services, interpreting services, psychological services, physical and occupational therapy, recreation, including therapeutic recreation, social work services, school nurse services designed to enable a child with a disability to receive a free appropriate public education as described in the individualized education program of the child, counseling services, including rehabilitation counseling, orientation and mobility services, and medical services, except that such medical services shall be for diagnostic and evaluation purposes only) as may be required to assist a child with a disability to benefit from special education, and includes the early identification and assessment of disabling conditions in children."

Exception: The term related service "does not include a medical device that is surgically implanted, or the replacement of such a device."

◆ *Significance*

A related service is available by right only if a child "needs" it in order to benefit from special education. The test is one of necessity, as under prior law. The 2004 amendments add interpreting services and school nurse services. Note again that a related service does not include an implanted medical device.

"Special education" means specially designed instruction, at no cost to parents, to meet the unique needs of a child with a disability, including–

1. instruction conducted in the classroom, in the home, in hospitals and institutions, and in other settings; and

2. instruction in physical education.

◆ *Significance*

No change from prior law; here is where IDEA provides for a "continuum" of service settings and thus gives some meaning to its Principle of the Least Restrictive Environment. Section 1412(a)(5) also implements the Principle and provides for a continuum of services.

"Specific learning disability."

1. In general the term "specific learning disability" means "a disorder in 1 or more of the basic psychological processes involved in understanding or in using language, spoken or written, which disorder may manifest itself in the imperfect ability to listen, think, speak, read, write, spell, or do mathematical calculations."

2. Disorders included: The term includes such conditions as "perceptual disabilities, brain injury, minimal brain dysfunction, dyslexia, and developmental aphasia."

3. Disorders excluded: The term does not include "a learning problem that is primarily the result of visual, hearing, or motor disabilities, of mental retardation, of emotional disturbance, or of environmental, cultural, or economic disadvantage."

◆ *Significance*

There is no change from prior law; the definition still uses an "inclusionary" approach (paragraphs 1 and 2) and an exclusionary approach (paragraph 3). In Section 1414(b)(6), IDEA identifies the standards that SEAs and LEAs may and may not use to evaluate a student to determine whether the student has a specific learning disability. See below under the Principle of Non-Discriminatory Evaluation.

"Supplementary aids and services" means "aids, services, and other supports that are provided in regular education classes or other education-related settings to enable children with disabilities to be educated with non-disabled children to the maximum extent appropriate in accordance with Section 1412(a)(5)."

◆ *Significance*
No change from prior law.

"Transition services" means "a coordinated set of activities for a child with a disability that–

1. "is designed to be within a results-oriented process, that is focused on improving the academic and functional achievement of the child with a disability from school to post-school activities, including post-secondary education, vocational education, integrated employment (including supported employment), continuing and adult education, adult services, independent living, or community participation;

2. "is based on the individual child's needs, taking into account the child's strengths, preferences and interests; and

3. "includes instruction, related services, community experiences, the development of employment and other post-school adult living objectives, and, when appropriate, acquisition of daily living skills and functional vocational evaluation."

◆ *Significance*
IDEA clearly is concerned about processes and procedures, but it also is focused on outcomes. Thus, a "results-oriented" process targets the students' academic and functional capacities. The emphasis on academic capacity-building is consistent with NCLB, and the emphasis on functional capacity-development acknowledges that academic development must accompany the development of other skills, namely those that enable students to achieve the four national policy goals: equal opportunity, full participation, independent living, and economic self-sufficiency. The addition of the term "results-oriented process" also means that school districts must provide, and may be held accountable

for not providing, these services, consistent with the NCLB Principle of Accountability and the IDEA Principle of Appropriate Education.

By referring to "community experiences," this section suggests that schools should be open to educating students in the real-life environments that they will experience when not in school; it is a call for education in "schools without walls."

Next, it declares that the outcomes that education offers to students without disabilities–employment and further education–should be available to students with disabilities as well. This definition expresses the notion of "high expectations" that constitutes one of the "busted barriers" we discussed above and that clearly aligns IDEA and NCLB with each other.

Finally, by focusing on outcomes, this section reflects educators' concerns that paperwork and process compliance have overtaken special education and must be minimized. See also Section 1411(e)(2)(c), authorizing state-level activities involving paperwork reduction, positive behavioral interventions and supports, mental health services, technology application, and other capacity building for SEAs and LEAs; and Section 1409, creating a paperwork reduction pilot program, and our comments about paperwork under the Principles of Non-Discriminatory Evaluation and Appropriate Education, below.

"Universal Design" has the meaning given the term under the Assistive Technology Act of 1998 (29 U.S.C. 3002).

◆ *Significance*
Universal design is a scientifically based method of adapting the curriculum and methods of instruction so that all students can benefit from education in the general curriculum. It is a technique that advances the Principle of Least Restrictive Environment (inclusion) and further aligns IDEA with NCLB.

"Ward of the State" means a child who is a foster child, ward of the state, or in the custody of a public welfare agency (does not include foster parent as defined above).

◆ *Significance*
These new provisions protect the rights and interests of children

16

who are wards of the state. This is important since access to due process remedies has been opened to "any party" under Section 1415(b)(6) and procedures are in place to appoint surrogates to act in place of the student's parents, Section 1415(b)(2).

Zero Reject: The First of the Six Principles

I. Reviewing the Six Principles

As we stated above, the six principles constitute a framework for understanding IDEA and organizing its provisions. So many people fail to understand IDEA wholly and conceptually because they lack a framework. With the framework of the six principles, however, all of IDEA makes sense as a sensible, seamless approach to educating students with disabilities: Enroll all, evaluate fairly, offer benefits, do it in the general education setting, be fair about what you do and how you settle your disputes, and be partners with parents and students. The Principle of Zero Reject commands the schools to enroll all and exclude none with disabilities. IDEA adopts several strategies to carry out this principle.

II. Ages Covered (3-21) Under Part B

Ages Covered, Section 1412(a)(1)(A): All students with disabilities, from ages 3 through 21, have a right to a free appropriate public education (FAPE), including those who have been suspended or expelled from school.

◆ *Significance of "Including" Language—No Cessation of Services*
By "including" disciplined students, IDEA creates a "no cessation" provision. See our discussion under "Discipline," below.

◆ *Significance and "Ineducability"*
"All means all." The term "all" includes even those students who, in the judgment of some people, seem to be "ineducable." In 1988, *Timothy W. v. Rochester School District* held that IDEA was enacted to ensure that all children with disabilities are provided an appropriate education. The court focused on the state's responsibility to the child, noting that Congress never intended to exclude any student. Instead, even if a student seems to be so

impaired that he cannot learn anything, the student still has the right to receive services from the SEA or LEA. The 2004 amendments restate the zero-reject foundation created by *Timothy W.* by continuing to require states to provide full educational opportunities to all children with disabilities between the ages of 3 and 21. Section 1412(a)(2).

◆ *Significance and Students with Contagious Diseases*
"All" also includes students with contagious diseases, such as HIV/AIDS, TB, or the like. Courts have consistently held that LEAs may not exclude these students but must educate them in environments and through methods that assure that their diseases will not infect other students or professionals.

◆ *Significance and Closing the Cracks, Section 1435(c)(5)(A)*
"All" refuses to allow any group of children or any individual child to "slip through the cracks." However, if preschoolers (ages 3 through 5, each inclusive) continue in Part C programs, they are not entitled to FAPE.

◆ *Significance and "High Risk Pool" Students, Section 1411(e)(3)*
LEAs may create a "risk pool" and "high cost fund" so that they may share their resources with each other to educate expensive-to-serve students. If an agency participates in a pool, it will have a hard time using the "cost" defense in a contest against parents who allege the LEA violated IDEA for their high-cost child.

III. Child Census, Section 1412(a)(3)

Section 1412 requires the SEA to assure that there will be an annual census of all students with disabilities (also known as "Child Find"):

> "All children with disabilities residing in the State, including children with disabilities who are homeless children or are wards of the State and children with disabilities attending private schools, regardless of the severity of their disabilities, and who are in need of special education and related services, are identified, located, and evaluated and a practical method is developed and implemented to determine which children with disabilities

are currently receiving needed special education and related services."

◆ *Significance*

This is a gap-closing provision that ensures that no children are denied FAPE because they are difficult to locate or serve. By targeting homeless students and those who are wards of the state (in state foster-care), IDEA acknowledges the problem of poverty and family structure, as it did in Section 1400(c)(10) with respect to limited English proficient and other minority (especially African American) students; IDEA thus transforms itself into a "welfare" statute as well as an education statute.

IV. Comprehensive Coverage, Section 1412

In order to serve the children found by the child census, Section 1412 also provides that every child who has a disability, regardless of the nature of the educational or other system that serves the child, is entitled to FAPE. This coverage includes students in religious schools, private schools, and charter schools.

> "To the extent consistent with the number and location of children with disabilities in the State who are enrolled by their parents in private elementary and secondary schools in the school district served by a local education agency, provision is made for the participation of those children in the program assisted or carried out under this part by providing for such children special education and related services..." Section 1412 (a)(10)(A)(i).

◆ *Significance in General*

IDEA does not extend all of its rights and benefits to all students in private schools. If a parent chooses to enroll the student in a private school, the SEA or LEA is required to provide only a proportionate amount of its Part B funds. If there are 1,000 students with disabilities in the SEA and there are 100 enrolled by parents in private schools, the SEA must provide only 10% of its Part B funds to allow those students to participate in the special education and related services that the LEA offers. Section 1412(a)(10)(A). If, on the other hand, an LEA places the student in a private school in order to discharge its IDEA duties to the student, then the LEA must pay for the private-school costs.

◆ *Significance for Parochial Schools*

This section, as well as Section 1412(a)(10)(A)(vi)(II), the "religious neutrality" provision, codifies two decisions of the United States Supreme Court. One held that an SEA or LEA does not violate the Federal Constitution's rule against "establishing" a religion when it provides related services to a student on the premises of a parochial school, *Zobrest v. Catalina Foothills School District*, 509 U.S. 1 (1993). The other held that it is not unconstitutional for an SEA or LEA to use public funds to support the tuition of students in parochial schools, *Zelman v. Simmons-Harris,* 536 U.S. 639 (2002). This provision and its related ones make it clear that parochial school students are entitled to IDEA's benefits and that the "wall" between church and state has been made smaller and lower so that parents may choose to make the spiritual value of a parochial education available to their children with disabilities. IDEA further provides that special education and related services provided to students whom parents place in private schools must be "secular, neutral, and non-ideological." Section 1412(10(A)(vi)(II). This provision mirrors the Court's non-proselytization interpretation of the church-state separation clause of the First Amendment.

◆ *Significance for Other Private Schools*

Under the 2004 amendments, children with disabilities enrolled in private schools by their parents are now more likely to be found by their local SEA or LEA because of (a) expanded requirements for child find processes, (b) required consultations with private school representatives, (c) required written confirmation that these consultations occurred, and (d) a right for private school officials to file a complaint with the SEA if an LEA does not make the appropriate effort to include their student population. Section 1412(a)(10)(A)(i)-(v).

◆ *Significance for Charter Schools*

The LEA must also serve students attending charter schools (public schools operating under a special authority from an SEA) in the same manner as students attending any other school; and the LEA must also provide funds to charter schools as any other school. Section 1413(a)(5).

◆ *Significance for Parent Choice*

Through its provisions related to parochial, private, and charter schools, IDEA allows parents to choose where to send their child and does not require the parents to run the risk that their child will lose the benefits of IDEA simply because of a placement into one of these kinds of schools.

V. Direct Services by State Educational Agency, Section 1413(g)

When an LEA fails to provide appropriate services to its students, the SEA must remedy the default by providing services directly to those students, using the funds that the LEA otherwise would have received.

◆ *Significance*
This section makes it possible for students in a defaulting LEA to get IDEA services from the SEA directly.

VI. Single-Agency Responsibility, Section 1412(a)(11)

The SEA is the state agency ultimately responsible for assuring that IDEA's requirements are carried out throughout the entire state. The SEA is responsible for interagency coordination to ensure that all students receive a free appropriate public education, including students those served by other state agencies, such as the state's mental health, developmental disabilities, or juvenile justice agencies. The 2004 amendments also add that the SEA is responsible for educating homeless children under the requirements of subtitle B of title VII of the McKinney-Vento Homeless Assistance Act (42 U.S.C. 11431 et seq.)

◆ *Significance*
As with the "direct services" provision, this provision assures that each student, wherever served, will receive IDEA's benefits.

VII. SEA Capacity-Building and Performance Goals, Section 1412(a)(12)-(25)

To secure outcome-based education and student progress, consistent with NCLB, the 2004 amendments require the SEA to:

1. deliver services in cooperation with other state agencies (12);
2. establish personnel qualifications (14);

3. establish performance goals and indicators for the SEA and LEA (15);

4. establish procedures for assessing students consistent with NCLB (16);

5. ensure financial oversight (17), (18), and (20);

6. ensure public participation in policy making (19) and (21);

7. account for discipline and report discipline data, including by race (22);

8. prevent over-identification of minority students (24);

9. build its instructional-materials capacity (23); and

10. prohibit SEAs and LEAs from requiring a student to take medication as a condition of attending school (25).

◆ *Significance of Capacity-Building Provisions*
These provisions build state and local capacity. Of special note are the new provisions related to discipline, minority-student over-representation, and mandatory medication. These are mirrored in the LEA obligations under Section 1413, as we note immediately below.

◆ *Significance of Medication Provision*
The 2004 amendments resolve a problem that arose because of the fact that many educators were suggesting to a student's parents that they should medicate their child, and because some educators were making the child's use of medication a condition of the child attending school. This amendment makes it clear that medication use may not be a condition of school enrollment.

VIII. LEA Capacity-Building, Section 1413

Because IDEA is a grant-in-aid of federal funds to SEAs and because the SEAs pass through the federal funds, with associated state funds, to LEAs (Section 1411), IDEA also requires LEAs to develop their capacities, principally by using IDEA funds, to comply with NCLB (Section 1413(a)(2)(D)), carry out a comprehensive program of personnel development (Section 1413(a)(3)), and use its funds flexibly for purposes related to NCLB, namely, early intervening services, high-cost services, case management, instructional materials, and migratory students (Section 1413(a)(4) and Section 1413(f)).

IX. Costs and Cost-Shifting, Section 1412(a)(12)(A)

The 2004 amendments allow for some of the costs of special education and related services to be "shifted" to or shared among other public agencies.

Section 1412(a)(12)(A) requires the SEA to assure that there is in effect "an interagency agreement or other mechanism for interagency coordination... between each public agency...and the State educational agency, in order to ensure that all services...that are needed to ensure a free appropriate public education are provided...."

Section 1412(a)(12)(A)(i) requires that "the financial responsibility of each public agency..., including the State Medicaid agency and other public insurers of children with disabilities, shall precede the financial responsibility of the local educational agency...."

Section 1412(a)(12)(B)(ii) requires all public agencies to fulfill their IDEA duties; if they do not, the SEA may carry out those duties and is specifically authorized to seek reimbursement for the costs of doing what the other agencies failed to do.

◆ *Significance*
These provisions assure that all agencies that have students with disabilities in their service systems must provide those students the benefits of IDEA. These provisions create a "first/last" payor system (other agencies pay first, the SEA pays last); and they spread the costs of special education and related services across more agencies than just the SEA. This provides greater education-related funding overall.

X. Architectural Barriers, Section 1404

The U.S. Secretary of Education may make grants to SEAs "to be used to acquire appropriate equipment, or to construct new facilities or alter existing facilities" to bring them into compliance with the "Americans with Disabilities Accessibility Guidelines for Buildings and Facilities".

◆ *Significance*
Without this section, zero reject would be difficult to achieve because architectural barriers would prohibit certain students from having access to school.

XI. Personnel, Section 1401(10) and Section 1412(a)(14)

IDEA seeks to build SEA and LEA capacity by assuring that all special education personnel will be highly qualified and, through Part D, to assure that there will be enough of them.

General Standards: Section 1401(10) defines "highly qualified" as the term applies to special education and related services staff. Section 1412(a)(14)(A) requires the SEA to set qualifications to ensure that school personnel are appropriately and adequately prepared and trained. The 2004 amendments add that personnel also must have the "content knowledge and skills to serve children with disabilities." This provision aligns IDEA with the NCLB Principle of Highly Qualified Teachers.

Related Services Personnel: Section 1412(a)(14)(B)(i) states that the qualifications under Section 1412(a)(14)(A) include qualifications for related service personnel that are consistent with any state certification, licensing, registration, or other requirements. The 2004 amendments add that related service personnel must meet the requirements of clause (i) and have not had certification or licensure requirements waived on an emergency, temporary, or provisional basis.

Paraprofessionals and Assistants: Section 1412(a)(14)(B)(iii) permits the SEA and LEAs to employ paraprofessionals if they are appropriately trained and supervised.

IDEA specifically provides for NCLB alignment by this provision: "The qualifications under [Section 1412(a)(14)(A)] shall also ensure that each person employed as a special education teacher in the State who teaches elementary school, middle school, or secondary school is highly qualified by the deadline established in section 1119(a)(2) of the Elementary and Secondary Education Act of 1965." Section 1412(a)(14)(C).

Personnel Vacancies: Section 1412(a)(14)(D) requires the SEA to require LEAs to take "measurable steps to recruit, hire, train, and retain highly qualified personnel" to meet the needs of children with disabilities.

◆ *Significance*
These sections assure that there will be a sufficient number of appropriately trained SEA and LEA personnel to carry out IDEA. They also align IDEA with the "highly qualified teacher" provisions under NCLB. The personnel are special and general educators, related service providers and paraprofessionals. Without this personnel, IDEA would make no real difference to the students; they would experience exclusion just as much as if they were not in school at all.

XII. Students in Correctional Facilities, Section 1412(a)(1)(B) and (11) and Section 1414(d)(7)

IDEA makes some exceptions to its Six Principles to take into account students who have been adjudicated.

Juvenile Offenders Treated as Adults: Section 1412(a)(1)(B)(ii) excludes from IDEA's benefits those juveniles who are incarcerated in an adult facility and who were not entitled to special education and did not have an IEP before they were incarcerated.

Other Juvenile Offenders: Section 1414(d)(7) also limits some of the IDEA rights of students with disabilities who had an IEP before they were incarcerated. These students do not have the right to participate in SEA or LEA assessments or to be provided transition programs if they will be over 21 when released from state custody. Also, if the SEA can demonstrate a "bona fide security or compelling penological interest that cannot otherwise be accommodated," the SEA may modify the IEP safeguards and the rules for placing the student in the least restrictive environment.

These provisions take into account that there are legitimate prison management or criminal rehabilitation reasons to restrict the IDEA rights of some students. At the same time, these provisions allow them to receive some of IDEA's benefits, consistent with the state's interest in confining, punishing, but yet rehabilitating them.

SEA Responsibility, Section 1412(a)(11)(C): The Governor may assign to a state agency other than the SEA the duties of carrying out IDEA for the benefit of students in state custody, Section 1412(a)(11)(C).

XIII. Discipline, Section 1415(k)

The 2004 amendments have rewritten and reorganized the discipline provisions previously found in Section 1415(k)(1)-(10). We discuss the details of these changes under Procedural Due Process, Part X.

XIV. Early Intervention (Ages 0-3) Under Part C, Section 1431 et seq.

A state may choose to provide services to infants and toddlers (birth/0 to 3) and their families. If a state chooses to provide these services, it will receive federal funds under IDEA's early intervention provisions, as authorized by Part C.

Early intervention is outcome-oriented and result-focused, for its purposes are:

1. "to enhance the development of infants and toddlers with disabilities, to minimize their potential for developmental delay, and to recognize the significant brain development that occurs during a child's first 3 years of life;

1. "to reduce the educational costs to our society, including our Nation's schools, by minimizing the need for special education and related services after infants and toddlers with disabilities reach school age;

1. "to maximize the potential for individuals with disabilities to live independently in society;

1. "to enhance the capacity of families to meet the special needs of their infants and toddlers with disabilities; and

1. "to enhance the capacity of State and local agencies and service providers to identify, evaluate, and meet the needs of all children, particularly minority, low-income, inner-city, and rural children, and infants and toddlers in foster care." Section 1431(a)(1)-(5).

◆ *Significance of EI as Prevention*
Early intervention is a preventive strategy that provides services for the child as well as the family in the critical, early years of the child's life–from birth to age 3.

◆ *Significance of EI as Aligned with National Goals*
The 2004 amendments include the goal that the SEA and LEA will "maximize" the potential of children with disabilities to live independently in society. This provision aligns early intervention with Part B.

◆ *Significance of EI as Family Centered*
As in the past, EI is centered on both the infant/toddler and the family.

◆ *Significance of EI as Capacity-Developing*
Part C seeks to develop the SEAs' and LEAs' capacity to provide early intervention. Part B (ages 3-21) does the same, consistent with the "barrier busting" and "solution-based" approaches that we described above.

Prolonged Early Intervention, Part C, Section 1435(c)(5)(A):
An SEA may develop a program under which parents whose child is eligible for services under section 1419 (ages 3-5) may elect to continue participation in Early Childhood. However, an LEA is not required to provide that child with FAPE under Part B.

XV. Transition Planning for Infants and Toddlers, Section 1412(a)(9)

In order to assure that infants and toddlers will make a smooth transition from early intervention (0-3 years) to early childhood (3-5 years), Section 1412(a)(9) requires a transition plan for them, consisting of interagency cooperation (early intervention and early childhood education in cooperation with each other) and an individualized education program, to be developed and implemented by the child's third birthday.

◆ *Significance*
No changes from prior law. Transition planning is a proactive initiative intended to provide a seamless transition from family-related services to education-related services. Parents may now invite a Part C service coordinator or other representative of the Part C program to the initial IEP meeting of their child to also help with transition. Section 1414(d)(1)(D).

Non-Discriminatory Evaluation: The Second of the Six Principles

I. Reviewing the Six Principles

After an LEA enrolls a student, consistent with the Principle of Zero Reject, it must comply with the Principle of Non-Discriminatory Evaluation and determine whether the student has a disability and, if so, what it must to do provide an appropriate education.

II. The NDE Team and the Purpose of the NDE, Section 1414(b)(4)

The Team: The NDE team consists of qualified professionals and the student's parents. Section 1414(b)(4). Practically speaking, persons who constitute the student's IEP team may also constitute the NDE team. Section 1414(d)(1)(B).

◆ *Significance*
This overlap in team membership led to the 2004 amendments allowing the LEA to encourage the consolidation of reevaluation meetings and other IEP meetings for the child. Section 1414(d)(3)(E).

The Purpose: The evaluation has two essential purposes, Section 1414(a)(1)(C) (i) and Section 1414(c)(1)(B), namely

1. to determine, in the case of an initial evaluation, whether the student has a disability (as defined in Section 1401) and, if so, what the student's educational needs are, (Section 1414(a)(1)(C)(i)) or in the case of a reevaluation, whether the student continues to have a disability and what the student's educational needs are, Section 1414(c)(1)(B)(i),

1. to determine further (Section 1414(c)(1)(B)(ii)-(iv)),

   a. the student's "present levels of academic achievement and related developmental needs of the child",

   a. "whether the child needs special education and related services, or in the case of a reevaluation of a child, whether the child continues to need special education and related services," and

   a. "whether any additions or modifications to the special education and related services are needed to enable the child to meet the measurable annual goals set out in the individualized education program of the child and to participate, as appropriate, in the general education curriculum."

◆ *Significance of Membership and Purpose*
As we just noted, this section links the non-discriminatory evaluation to the individualized education program and the student's placement in two ways; first, by having essentially the same people serve on the evaluation and on the IEP/placement teams and, second, by making the evaluation's purposes explicit and requiring them to be connected to program and placement. Thus, evaluation is the basis for determining not only whether the student has a disability but also, if that is the case, what the school must do about that fact (namely, develop and carry out an appropriate education through the IEP and provide services in the least restrictive environment of the general curriculum). The 2004 amendments make clear that an evaluation is meant to determine how a disability affects a student's educational needs. It thus confines the overall function of the IDEA to meeting the student's educational needs, not the student's or family's other needs, however much they may affect the student's education.

III. Evaluation Standards and Procedures, Section 1414(b)

In order to be sure that the student has a disability and what the student needs in general and special education, the NDE team must adhere to specific standards and procedures, including those related to

1. the student:

    a. the student must be evaluated for two purposes, namely to determine whether the student has a disability and the content of the child's individualized education program, "including information related to enabling the

        child to be involved in and progress in the general education curriculum, or, for preschool children, to participate in appropriate activities..." Section 1414(b)(2)(A).

1. the assessments, Section 1414(b)(3):

    a. must be "selected and administered so as not to be discriminatory on a racial or cultural basis," Section 1414(b)(3)(A)(i),

    a. must be "provided and administered in the language and form most likely to yield accurate information on what the child knows and can do academically, developmentally, and functionally, unless it is not feasible to so provide or administer," Section 1414(b)(3)(A)(ii),

    a. must be "used for purposes for which the assessments or measures are valid and reliable," Section 1414(b)(3)(A)(iii),

    a. must be "administered by trained and knowledgeable personnel," Section 1414(b)(3)(A)(iv), and

    a. must be "administered in accordance with any instructions provided by the producer of such assessments," Section 1414(b)(3)(A)(v).

1. the evaluation process, Section 1414(b)(2), must:

   a. include "a variety of assessment tools and strategies to gather relevant functional, developmental, and academic information, including information provided by the parent, that may assist" the team in making the two critical determinations (does the student have a disability; if so, what should the student's education consist of), Section 1414(b)(2)(A),

   a. not rely on "any single measure or assessment as the sole criterion for determining whether the child is a child with a disability or determining an appropriate educational program for the child," Section 1414(b)(2)(B), and

   a. "use technically sound instruments" to assess the student across four domains, namely, cognitive, behavioral, physical, and developmental, Section 1414(b)(2)(C).

1. in conducting the initial and subsequent reevaluations, the IEP team must, under Section 1414 (c)(1):

   a. "review existing evaluation data on the child, including evaluations and information provided by the parents of the child, current classroom-based, local or State assessments, and classroom-based observations, and observations by teachers and related services providers"; and

   a. on the basis of that review, and input from the child's parents, "identify what additional data, if any, are needed" to reach the required conclusions about disability and special education needs.

◆ *Significance of Standards and Procedures*
A typical approach of the law is to require standards by which certain consequences are measured, and procedures for applying the standards. IDEA's NDE principle adopts the standard of a fair evaluation: The evaluation may not be biased because of race, culture, or language; and the instruments that the team uses for

the evaluation must be "validated" for the purposes for which they are used, and must be "technically sound" for evaluating the student in each of four domains. The requirement for "validated" and "technically sound" instruments reflects the NCLB emphasis on scientifically based interventions, including evaluations that lead to special education.

Moreover, IDEA's NDE principle adopts the procedures approach by requiring the team to use more than one instrument and to take into account existing evaluation data from different sources.

Together, these NDE standards and procedures assure that the LEA will accurately identify the student as having a disability and then will develop an appropriate individualized education for the student, to be provided in the least restrictive environment. The

team will accomplish those two purposes on the basis of the evaluation and on no other basis. Thus, the evaluation is the foundation for all that follows.

The evaluation must focus on four domains that affect a student's education–cognitive, behavioral, physical, and developmental domains. Further, the evaluation team must consider existing evaluation data, but it has an option not to do a complete reevaluation each time some reevaluation has to be done.

IV. Exclusion from Special Education

In determining whether a student qualifies for IDEA benefits, the NDE team must apply certain exclusionary standards. Those standards (or criteria) safeguard against erroneous classification into special education.

Determinant Factor, Section 1414(b)(5): The team may not determine that the student has a disability "if the determinant factor for such determination is lack of appropriate instruction in reading, including in the essential components of reading instruction (as defined in section 1208(3) of the Elementary and Secondary Education Act of 1965); lack of instruction in math; or limited English proficiency."

◆ *Significance of Determinant Factor*
By incorporating the reading instruction definition from NCLB,

the 2004 amendments have essentially set forth substantive standards (criteria) for exclusion from special education. This section assures that children from language-minority groups or from educationally impoverished programs will not be made eligible for IDEA solely because of those factors. The new language reflects a continuing concern with the over-representation of minority students in special education and seeks to reduce their representation in special education.

Special Rule for Specific Learning Disability, Section 1414(b)(6): This new provision links to the definition of "specific learning disability" in Section 1402(30). It provides that an LEA is not required to take into account whether the student has a "severe discrepancy between achievement and intellectual ability in oral expression, listening comprehension, written expression, basic reading skill, reading comprehension, mathematical calculation, or mathematical reasoning." The LEA may, however, use a "severe discrepancy" standard; it is simply not required to do so. Further, the LEA may but is not required to use a "process that determines if the child responds to scientific, research-based intervention."

◆ *Significance of the Special Rule*
The section seems to discourage the discrepancy standard and to encourage the scientifically based intervention standard, consistent with NCLB.

V. Initial Evaluations, Section 1414(a)(1)

Either a parent, an SEA, other state agency, or an LEA may initiate a request for an initial evaluation to determine if the child is a child with a disability. The initial evaluation must be done within 60 days after the agency receives the consent of the student's parents for the evaluation, or, if the state establishes a different timeframe within which the evaluation must be conducted, within that timeframe.

◆ *Significance*
The 2004 amendments add to the list of individuals or entities that may request an initial evaluation and also add the timeframe. IDEA does not define "other state agency." Such an agency might be a child welfare and protective services agency serving "wards

of the state" in foster care, or a juvenile justice agency that has responsibility for a student adjudicated for committing a crime.

VI. Parent Participation, Section 1414(d)(1)(B)

The student's parents must be members of the evaluation and IEP teams.

VII. Parental Consent, Section 1414(a)(1)(D)

Any agency proposing to conduct an initial evaluation or any subsequent evaluation must obtain the "informed consent" of the child's parents before conducting the evaluation or reevaluation.

The parents' consent applies only to that particular evaluation and "shall not be construed as consent for placement for receipt of special education and related services."

If the parents do not consent to an initial evaluation or do not respond to a request to provide consent, the LEA may use mediation or due process procedures to secure approval for an evaluation or reevaluation. (We explain those procedures below under Part Six, the Principle of Procedural Due Process.) If the student's parents refuse to consent to the student receiving special education and related services or if the parents fail to respond to the agency's request for consent, then, under Section 1414(a)(1)(D)(ii):

1. the LEA shall not provide any special education or related services to the child by pursuing mediation or due process;

2. the LEA shall not be considered to be in violation of the requirement to make available a free appropriate public education to the student because it has not provided the student with the special education and related services for which the LEA has requested the parents' consent; and

3. the LEA shall not be required to convene an IEP meeting or develop an IEP for the student in order to provide the special education services for which the LEA has requested the parent's consent.

◆ *Significance of Parental Veto*
The 2004 amendments clearly state that "no means no." Once a parent decides that the student will not participate in special education, the LEA may not put the child into special education or provide any special education services to the student under IDEA.

The 2004 amendments also absolve the LEA from any further responsibility and obligations to provide special education and related services. The LEA does not even have to pursue due process to receive authority to provide services for the child.

Thus, parents have been given direct responsibility for their child's education. Their decision affects the student's current programming, because, if the parents do not consent to an evaluation, the LEA can claim that it is not charged with IDEA responsibility to the student. It then may proceed with discipline and other general education consequences, accordingly.

There is, however, one other route that a parent may take to assure that the student receives some benefit in school, and it is to assert that the student has a disability under Section 504 and ADA and that the LEA must offer "reasonable accommodations" to the student. If the parent goes the "504/ADA route," after rejecting IDEA benefits, the parent will have to prove, through evaluations, that the student meets the definition of "disabled" under those laws. That may be difficult for the parent to do, given the parent's choice not to have the student qualify under IDEA.

4. If the LEA or other agency is proposing to conduct a reevaluation, it must secure the parents' consent, but if it cannot do so, it may proceed with the evaluation if it can "demonstrate that it had taken reasonable measures to obtain such consent and the child's parent has failed to respond." Section 1414(c)(3).

◆ *Significance of Parental Default*
Parent participation in the evaluation process is critical, assuring (a) collaborative decision-making; (b) parental involvement in the child's education; (c) parental information that aids the other members of the team; and (d) parental knowledge about whether the child has a disability and, if so, what the child's program and placement will be (with the evaluation as a foundation). With at least one parent as a member of the team and with IDEA's

requirement for parental consent, the evaluation process can focus on each area of the child's educational needs and each area of concern for the parents. The contrary also is true: The uninvolved or uninformed parent causes the student to pay the price of the parent's inaction or ignorance. That fact alone significantly increases parents' responsibility for choosing wisely, for accepting the consequences of their choices, and for involving themselves in the entire evaluation process.

VIII. Reevaluation, Section 1414(a)(2)

The 2004 amendments simplify the reevaluation requirements.

Mandatory and Optional Reevaluation: The team must conduct a reevaluation if:

1. the LEA determines that the educational or related-services needs, including improved academic achievement and functional performance, of the child warrant a reevaluation; or

2. the parents or a teacher request a reevaluation.

Otherwise, the LEA does not have to conduct a reevaluation.

If a reevaluation is to be conducted, it–

1. may not occur more frequently than once a year, unless the parent and the local LEA agree otherwise; and

2. must occur at least once every three years, unless the parent and the LEA agree that a reevaluation is unnecessary.

◆ *Significance of Discretionary and Mandatory Reevaluation*
The 2004 amendments clarify that a reevaluation may be conducted to determine if the student has improved both academically and functionally and no longer requires special education. This is a discretionary reevaluation. Discretionary reevaluations become mandatory only on two conditions: either the LEA wants one because the student's academic achievement and functional performance has changed (including by improvement), or the parent or a teacher asks for a reevaluation.

The 2004 amendments also provide that the reevaluation may not be done twice in one year unless the SEA and parents agree, and that the LEA and parents may waive the three-year reevaluation.

Clearly, the 2004 amendments seek to reduce the amount of "paperwork burden" that reevaluations allegedly have caused.

Parental Consent, Section 1414(c)(3): Reevaluation requires parental consent.

No Reevaluation if Graduating or Aging Out, Section 1414(c)(5)(B): LEAs no longer have to perform a reevaluation before they terminate a student's IDEA eligibility because the student will graduate from secondary school with a regular diploma, or because the student will exceed the age eligibility for a free appropriate public education under state law.

Instead, the LEA has to provide a summary of the child's academic achievement and functional performance, including recommendations on how to assist the child in meeting any post-secondary goals.

◆ *Significance*
This provision reduces the paperwork burden on the LEA but provides for educational data to be available for post-school purposes (namely, those related to transition and the four IDEA outcomes).

Standards/Criteria and Procedures for Reevaluation Same as for Initial Evaluation, Section 1414(a) and Section 1414(c): The evaluation/IEP team must comply with all of the standards and procedures that apply to the initial evaluation, namely those in Section 1414(a) and Section 1414(c). An LEA must follow the (a) and (c) standards and procedures before determining that a student is "no longer a child with a disability." The exception to this rule occurs when the student is graduating with a "regular diploma" or "is exceeding the age eligibility" for IDEA benefits (under state law). Section 1414(c)(5)(B).

Additional Procedures for Reevaluation, Section 1414(c)(1)-(4):
During each reevaluation, the team must

1. examine existing evaluation data, (i.e. classroom-based, local, or state assessments, classroom-based observations, parent input),

2. identify what additional data, if any, are needed to determine whether the student continues to have a disability or special educational needs, and the student's present levels of academic achievement and related developmental needs,

3. notify the student's parents that no new data are needed and why that is so (so no new reevaluation is warranted), and

4. conduct new reevaluations only upon parental request.

◆ *Significance of "Educational Needs" Language*
As we noted above, the reevaluation section generally provides an opportunity for the LEA or the parents to request more evaluations if it appears that the student's educational needs are unmet, including, for example, because the student has new needs or because some of the student's needs had not been officially identified. That makes sense: unmet needs justify further evaluation.

The 2004 amendments clarify that these evaluations are meant to determine the student's "educational need." It is possible for a student to have disability-related needs that are not connected to the student's education; those needs do not interfere with the student's ability to learn in the general education setting and therefore do not require special education. Since the role of the SEA and LEA is to "educate," the reevaluation, like the initial evaluation, focuses on the student's educational needs only.

IX. No Evaluation, No Services, Section 1414(a)(1)

An agency may not provide special education and related services without conducting a full and individual initial evaluation.

◆ *Significance for Misclassification*
This section ensures that an agency (SEA, LEA, or other public agency) will not erroneously place a student who does not need

special education into special education. It guards against misclassification and against the possibility that an agency will seek to remove the student from general education for reasons that do not relate to the student's need for special education. Any misclassification or improper placement not only can damage the student and impair the student's opportunity for an education and adult life chances, but can also dilute the funds and staff available for students who have genuine, documented (evaluated) special educational needs.

◆ *Significance of "Positive Behavioral Support" and "Mental Health" Services*
An SEA may spend some of its Part B money to assist LEAS to provide positive behavioral interventions and "appropriate mental health services" to students with disabilities. Section 1411(e)(2)(c). It seems that an LEA that offers these services must do so on the basis of the non-discriminatory evaluation, because evaluation links to programs. It also seems that the services must relate to the student's "educational needs" and that a parent must consent to them, especially any mental health services, simply because parent consent for mental health services is usually required by state law.

◆ *Significance of Exception for "Early Intervening Services"*
An LEA also may spend some of its Part B money to offer "early intervening services" to students who are not formally classified under IDEA but who need "additional academic and behavioral support to succeed in a general education environment." Section 1413(f). These services may include interagency financing structures, professional development, and educational and behavioral evaluations, services, and supports, including "scientifically based literacy instruction." The students who receive these services are not entitled to any other benefits under IDEA, including the non-discriminatory evaluation or an appropriate education (with an IEP). Accordingly, parental consent for those services is not required, at least not under IDEA.

X. Independent Evaluations, Section 1415(b)(1)

A parent who disagrees with the findings of an LEA's initial evaluation or reevaluation has the right to obtain an independent evaluation of the child.

◆ *Significance*

An area of significant dispute concerning independent evaluations is whether the LEA or the parent should bear the cost of the independent evaluation. A parent may request that a school pay for an independent evaluation, but the school may avail itself of due process procedures to show that its evaluations were appropriate and valid and that it therefore is not required to pay for them.

XI. Infants and Toddlers, Section 1435(a)(3)

The non-discriminatory evaluation requirement extends to infants and toddlers (birth/0 to 3).

◆ *Significance*

This section protects infants and toddlers from misclassification.

Appropriate Education:
The Third of the Six Principles

I. Reviewing the Six Principles

After an LEA enrolls a student (zero reject) and applies the proper standards and procedures to determine that the student has a disability (non-discriminatory evaluation), the LEA must provide the student with a genuine opportunity to learn (appropriate education). But just what is an "appropriate education" or what is a genuine opportunity to benefit? IDEA answers those questions by setting out standards and procedures that include creating an individually tailored plan, called the student's Individualized Education Program (IEP) or, in the case of an infant/toddler, the Individualized Family Service Plan (IFSP).

II. Defining an Appropriate Education, Section 1401(9)

Section 1401(9) defines the term "Free Appropriate Public Education" as: "Special education and related services that have been provided at public expense, under public supervision and direction, and without charge; meet the standards of the State educational agency; include an appropriate preschool, elementary school, or secondary school education in the State involved;

and are provided in conformity with the individualized education program."

III. Interpreting the Definition: The *Rowley* Decision

The U.S. Supreme Court's first special education decision, *Board of Education v. Rowley*, 458 U.S. 176 (1982), defined "appropriate" and the 2004 amendments do nothing to change the Court's approach. The Court adopted a two-part approach to defining "appropriate."

One part holds that "appropriate" consists of a program that provides the student with a reasonable opportunity to benefit. This is the "benefit" standard.

The second part holds that an "appropriate" education results from following IDEA's procedures, specifically by conducting a non-discriminatory evaluation, developing an individualized education program, attempting to place the child in the least restrictive appropriate program, assuring that the parents have access to the child's school records throughout this process, and convening a due process hearing if the parents wish to protest the placement or any other action related to the child's right to a free appropriate public education. This is the "process" standard.

IDEA continues to define "appropriate," consistent with *Rowley*, by requiring that the student benefit and that the IDEA procedures be followed. The keystones to "appropriate" are, of course, the non-discriminatory evaluation (because it is the basis for the IEP), the IEP (which is the basis for the student's curriculum, related services, supplementary aids and services), and the student's placement in the least restrictive environment that is appropriate for the student.

IV. Individualized Education Program (IEP), Section 1414(d)

The IEP is a written statement that includes:

1. "a statement of the student's present levels of academic achievement and functional performance, including

   a. "how the student's disability affects the child's involvement and progress in the general education curriculum;

   b. "for preschool children, as appropriate, how the disability affects the child's participation in appropriate activities; and

   c. "for students with disabilities who take alternate assessments aligned to alternate achievement standards, a description of benchmarks or short-term objectives"

◆ *Significance of These Three Elements of the IEP*
The 2004 amendments emphasize "academic and functional performance," consistent with NCLB and the "high expectations" theme of IDEA and NCLB. They also connect the student's education with the general education curriculum, consistent with NCLB's thesis that all students should be assessed and with IDEA's Principle of the Least Restrictive Environment. Finally, they acknowledge that some students will take "alternative assessments," consistent with NCLB, but they provide that these students and no others must have an IEP that sets out benchmarks and short-term objectives. The IEP of every other IDEA student may contain benchmarks and short-term objectives but is not required to do so.

2. "a statement of measurable annual goals, including academic and functional goals, to

   a. "meet the student's needs that result from the student's disability to enable the student to be involved in and make progress in the general education curriculum; and

   b. "meet each of the child's other educational needs that result from the disability"

◆ Significance of "Meet the Educational Needs" Language

Here again, the 2004 amendments focus on academic and functional goals, accountability for those goals' attainment, placement in the general curriculum (least restrictive environment), and meeting the student's educational needs (but only those needs), as identified by the non-discriminatory evaluation.

3. "a description of how the student's progress toward meeting the annual goals will be measured" and when periodic reports on the student's progress toward meeting the annual goals (such as through the use of quarterly or other periodic reports, concurrent with the issuance of report cards) will be provided

◆ Significance of the "Progress" Language

Here too, the 2004 amendments connect to the NCLB requirements for periodic reporting.

4. "a statement of the special education and related services and supplementary aids and services, based on peer-reviewed research to the extent practicable", to be provided to the student, or on the student's behalf, and a statement of the "program modifications or supports for school personnel that will be provided" so that the student may–

   a. "advance appropriately toward attaining the annual goals;"

   b. "be involved in and make progress in the general education curriculum" and "participate in extracurricular and other non-academic activities;" and

   c. "be educated and participate with other children with disabilities and non-disabled children in (those) activities"

◆ Significance of the "Peer-Reviewed" Language

The 2004 amendments repeat the language of the previous IDEA but add that the services and aids must be " based on peer reviewed research to the extent practicable," thus, once again, linking IDEA to the NCLB Principle of Scientifically Based Intervention.

5. "an explanation of the extent, if any," to which the student will not participate with non-disabled children in the regular classroom and in the general education curriculum, extracurricular activities, and other non-academic activities

◆ *Significance of the "If Any" Language*
This is the same language as in the previous IDEA. It requires the LEA to justify separating the student from the three domains of the least restrictive environment (general education curriculum, extracurricular activities and non-academic activities).

6. a statement of:

   a. any individual appropriate accommodations that are necessary to measure the student's academic achievement and functional performance on state and district-wide assessments [including assessments under required under NCLB] and;

   b. if the IEP team determines that the student shall take an alternate assessment on a particular state or district-wide assessment of student achievement, a statement of why the student cannot participate in the regular assessment and a statement identifying the particular alternate assessment that the team selects as appropriate for the child

◆ *Significance of the "Assessment" Language*
The connection with the NCLB Principle of Accountability is explicit. Indeed, the presumption is that IDEA students will be subject to the "regular assessments" but that presumption may be overturned only for good cause as set out in the student's IEP. There are several types of assessments, and the student's IEP will identify the appropriate one: the regular assessment without modifications, the regular assessment with modifications, an alternate assessment tied to the same standards as for non-disabled students, and an alternate assessment tied to different standards.

7. the projected date for the beginning of services and modifications and the anticipated frequency, location, and duration of those services and modifications

8. beginning no later than the first IEP to be in effect when the student is 16, and updated annually thereafter:

   a. "appropriate measurable post-secondary goals, based upon age appropriate transition assessments related to training, education, employment and where appropriate, independent living skills"

◆ *Significance of "Age 16" Language and Transition Outcomes*

The 2004 amendments have raised the age for transition planning from 14 to 16 and emphasized that transition planning should be related to training, education, employment, and independent living skills. This change directly reflects the IDEA policy outcomes of "helping children with disabilities achieve equality of opportunity, full participation, independent living and economic sufficiency" and preparing them to lead "productive and independent lives." Section 1400 (c)(1).

   b. the transition services (including courses of study) needed to assist the student in reaching those goals; and

   c. beginning no later than one year before the student reaches the age of majority under state law, a statement that the student has been informed of his/her rights under IDEA, if any, that will transfer to the student when the student reaches the age of majority.

◆ *Significance of the IEP in a Global Sense*

It is worth repeating that the IEP is explicitly connected with and serves as the nexus between the non-discriminatory evaluation, the student's program, and the student's least restrictive environment placement ("involvement and progress in the general education curriculum"). In addition, the IEP provisions are significant because:

   • They make clear that educational performance consists of both academic achievement and functional performance. They link academic performance to the four national policy goals and to adult outcomes (and that is the premise of the NCLB Principle of Accountability), but they also value functional performance because how a student functions as an adult determines whether the student will be entitled to the protections of Section 504 and ADA.

- They secure accountability by identifying the student's present educational levels and measurable annual goals; by presuming that the student will participate in state and local assessments, including those required under NCLB, and thus be "measured" according to how he or she is doing relative to other students; and by requiring schools to notify parents (as often as they notify parents of non-disabled students) about their child's progress.

- They emphasize that, if a student cannot participate in the assessments, the IEP team must justify why the student cannot participate in the regular assessment and must also validate the choice of alternate assessments.

- They assure related services and supplementary aids and services so the student can benefit from special education and participate in the general education curriculum, extracurricular activities, and other non-academic activities.

- They create a presumption in favor of a general education curriculum placement and require the IEP team to justify any other placement.

- They emphasize transition to adulthood and self-determination by the new provisions that "devolve" or transfer the parents' rights to act for the student to the student himself or herself.

V. The Individualized Education Program Team, Section 1414(d)(1)(B) consists of

1. the student's parents,

2. not less than one general education teacher of the student, if the student is or may be participating in the general education environment,

3. not less than one special education teacher, or where appropriate, not less than one provider of special education to the student,

4. a representative of the local agency who is qualified to provide or supervise specially designed instruction to

meet the unique needs of students with disabilities and is knowledgeable about the general education curriculum and the availability of local agency resources,

5. an individual who can interpret the instructional implications of evaluation results (who may be a member of the team already), and

6. at the parents' or agency's discretion, other individuals who have knowledge or special expertise (including related services personnel), and the student (when appropriate).

◆ *Significance of Membership*

The NDE team and the IEP team have overlapping, common members, thus assuring a link between evaluation data and program and placement decisions. More than that, the team members are expert in evaluation, special education programming, special education administration, general education curriculum, and local resources that can support the student's placement into the general education program. By having a team consisting of these individuals, IDEA assures a more robust and holistic evaluation and decision-making processes geared toward "benefit" in the general curriculum.

VI. Parent Participation

The LEA must take specific steps to ensure that the student's parents are members of the evaluation and IEP teams. These steps include

1. advance notice of meetings

2. mutually convenient scheduling

3. interpreters when necessary (the parents may have language, sight, or hearing limitations)

4. meeting without parent participation only where attempts to include parents have failed

5. allowing parent(s) to participate by videoconference and conference calls. Section 1414(f).

◆ *Significance*

Each LEA must make a good faith effort to secure parental

participation; otherwise, valuable information about the student may not be considered.

VII. IEP Team Attendance, Section 1414 (d)(1)(C)

An IEP team member is not required to attend all or even part of an IEP meeting if the student's parents and the LEA agree that the member's attendance "is not necessary because the member's area of the curriculum or related services is not being modified or discussed at the meeting."

Further, a team member may be excused from attending all or part of an IEP meeting even when the meeting involves a modification to or discussion of the member's area of the curriculum or related services. The parents and the LEA must consent to the excusal, and the member must submit, in writing to the parent and the IEP Team, input into the development of the IEP, filed prior to the meeting. Note that the parents' agreement and consent must be in writing.

In the case of a child who was served under the Early Childhood Program (Part C), the parent may request that the Part C service coordinator or other representative come to the initial meeting to ensure a smooth transition. Section 1414 (d)(1)(D).

◆ *Significance*
This new provision reflects Congress' attempt to reduce the paperwork and the time-cost that schools have complained about. Again, parents will have to be extremely well informed to either (a) agree or disagree that a certain related service or curriculum area should or should not be changed before an actual IEP meeting or (b) consent or refuse to consent to the excusal of the team member who submits his/her proposal in writing.

VIII. Required Considerations, Section 1414(d)(3)(A)

In developing the IEP, the team must consider

1. the student's strengths, parental concerns, all evaluation results, and the student's academic, developmental and functional needs; and

2. "special factors", as follows:

    a. in the case of a student "whose behavior impedes the child's learning or that of others," the IEP team must "consider the use of positive behavioral interventions and supports, and other strategies, to address that behavior"

◆ *Significance of "Impeding" Language*

IDEA does not define "impede" but leaves it to the IEP team to define and operationalize the term as it applies to the particular student. Under the 2004 amendments, no longer is the phrase "when appropriate" included as a qualification or limitation on when the IEP team must consider positive behavioral interventions and supports (PBS). This is a logical change, since when would it not be appropriate to use positive interventions if a student's behavior affects his/her learning or the learning of others? Now, if the student's behavior "impedes," the team "must consider the use of positive behavioral interventions and supports, and other strategies." This phrasing creates a presumption in favor of using positive behavioral support interventions, strategies, and supports; but it does not rule out other types of interventions and indeed requires the team to consider other strategies as well.

What is the purpose of the "consider" requirement? It is to prod the team to create a program that will prevent the behaviors from occurring, replace them with more appropriate behaviors, or both. It also encourages intervention and prevention so the student can benefit from special education and progress toward the national policy goals. That is why IDEA uses the term "to address that behavior."

    b. "in the case of a child with limited English proficiency, consider the language needs of the child as such needs relate to the child's IEP"

◆ *Significance of the "LEP" Language*

Some children in special education may need bilingual education, too. Therefore, the IEP team must consider whether bilingual education would benefit the student.

    c. "in the case of a child who is blind or visually impaired, provide for instruction in Braille and use of Braille unless the IEP Team determines, after an evaluation of the child's reading and writing skills, needs, and appropriate reading and writing media (including an evaluation of the child's future needs for instruction in Braille or the use of Braille), that instruction in Braille or the use of Braille is not appropriate for the child"

◆ *Significance of the Visual Impairment Language*
This provision creates a presumption in favor of Braille training but it does not mandate inappropriate use of Braille training.

> d. for all students and particularly "in the case of a child who is deaf or hard of hearing, consider the child's language and communication needs, opportunities for direct communications with peers and professional personnel in the child's language and communication mode, academic level, and full range of needs, including opportunities for direct instruction in the child's language and communication mode"

◆ *Significance of the "Communication" Language*
This provision suggests that children who use similar languages because of their linguistic hearing impairments should be grouped with each other in order to facilitate communication amongst each other and with teachers.

> e. for all students, "consider whether the child needs assistive technology devices and services."

◆ *Significance of the "AT" Language*
Assistive technology is a related service and can be useful to many students; the IEP team must rule it in or out for each child.

IX. Special Duties of Regular Educator, Section 1414(d)(3)(C)

A regular education teacher of the student, when participating as a member of the IEP Team, "shall, to the extent appropriate, participate in the development of the IEP of the child, including the determination of appropriate positive behavioral interventions and supports and other strategies and the determination of supplementary aids and services, program modifications, and support for school personnel..."

◆ *Significance for LRE and Inclusion*
The general educator not only must participate in IEP development but also must especially attend to the "impede/ positive supports" provision, and help the team determine the supplementary aids and services for the student and the appropriate program modifications and supports for the general educators and special educators. However, it remains unclear how this will be implemented in light of the team member attendance waiver if "the member's area of the curriculum" will not be discussed.

X. Private School Placement and IEPs, Section 1412(a)(10)(B)

An SEA or LEA that places a student in a private school is still responsible for implementing the student's IEP.

◆ *Significance*
This requirement links to the Principle of Zero Reject. When an SEA or LEA places a student in a private school, it does so in order to provide the student with an appropriate education. Therefore, it must ensure that the private school implements the student's IEP. Otherwise, the placement would result in the student not receiving the full benefit of IDEA, thereby violating the Zero Reject Principle.

XI. Waiver of Team Meetings for Changes and Amendments, Section 1414(d)(3)(D)

The parents and the LEA may agree not to convene an IEP meeting to make changes after they develop the student's annual IEP and during that same school year. Instead, they may develop a written document to amend or modify the child's current IEP.

The LEA must also encourage the consolidation of the reevaluation meeting and other IEP team meetings. Section 1414 (d)(3)(E).

Changes to the IEP may be made either by the entire IEP Team or by amending the IEP rather than redrafting the entire document.

Upon request, a parent must be provided with a revised copy of the IEP with the amendments incorporated.

◆ *Significance for Team*
These three new provisions clearly address the issue of paperwork reduction and LEA time management. They require continued cooperation among team members but waive face-to-face meetings upon the consent of both the parents and the LEA. Note that a pilot program provides the opportunity for states to allow parents and LEAs the opportunity for long-term planning and the option of developing a comprehensive multiyear IEP that would be in effect for three years. Section 1414(d)(5)

XII. Revising the IEP, Section 1414(d)(4)

The LEA must establish or revise the IEP as necessary, but at least annually, to determine that the student's IEP goals are being met. If they are not being met, the LEA must revise the IEP to address:

1. any lack of expected student progress toward the annual goals, and in the general education curriculum, where appropriate,

2. the results of any non-discriminatory evaluation,

3. information about the child provided to or by the parents,

4. the student's anticipated future needs, or

5. any other matters.

For a student currently in special education, the LEA must conduct the review early enough to ensure that all revisions are in effect by the beginning of the next school year. Section 1414(d)(2)(A).

◆ *Significance*
In addition to parent and general educator participation, these provisions assure periodic review with a focus on timeliness, access to and benefit from general education, and use of non-discriminatory evaluation data.

XIII. Related and Other Services and Supports, Section 1414(d)(1)(A)(i)(4)

This section requires the IEP team to specify (a) which related services the student needs to benefit from special education; (b) which supplementary aids and services the student needs to participate in and progress through the general curriculum; and (c) what program modifications or supports for school personnel will be provided so that the student can participate in and benefit from general and special education.

◆ *Significance of Related Services for Health Issues*
This provision marshals a wide range of services to the benefit of the student and the school's special and general educators; it thus supports placement in the least restrictive environment, consistent with that IDEA principle. Note that Congress made clear that "related services" do not include implanted medical devices. Congress did not, however, do anything else to clarify the meaning of related services as they affect a student's health, and thus Congress leaves intact the two related-service decisions of the United States Supreme Court.

The Supreme Court first clarified the meaning of a related service in *Irving Independent School District v. Tatro,* 468 U.S. 883 (1984). There, the Court looked at two crucial factors to determine whether a service is "related" or is a "medical service" that is not a related service: (a) whether the service in question is a supportive service that enables the student to benefit from special education; and (b) whether the service in question is a medical service that has purposes other than educational diagnosis or evaluation. The Court held that the service in *Tatro,* clean intermittent catheterization, is a related and supportive service because, without it, the student could not attend school and thereby benefit from special education. Clean intermittent catheterization also is not a medical service because it can be administered by a nurse and because school nurses are clearly required by Congress under the "school health service" component of "related services." The test of "related" vs. "medical" service is, in the last analysis, based on whether the service is or may legally be performed by a person other than a physician or other than under a physician's direct supervision and authority; whether the service is simple, has a low cost to the LEA but high benefit to the student; is not "merely" life-sustaining but also has educational value; is typically provided in school as distinguished from a hospital or medical clinic; and is performed by a person who may do that service without special licensure and without violating the state laws on medical and nursing practice.

Fifteen years later, the Court, in *Cedar Rapids Community School District v. Garrett F.,* 526 U.S. 66 (1999), affirmed its two-step analysis in *Tatro* by holding that the District must provide "related services" that included nursing services during the school day in order to "help guarantee that students like Garrett are integrated into the public schools." Garrett F. needed assistance with urinary bladder catheterization once a day, the suctioning of his tracheotomy tube and assistance in breathing when his ventilator was checked for functioning. The Court held that these services qualified as supportive services because Garrett F. could not attend school without them and because they did not need to be performed by a physician.

The new provisions for "high cost" and "risk pool" activities by the SEA and LEA should aid LEAs that find that they face huge expenses to comply with IDEA and these cases.

XIV. Transition Services, Section 1401(34), Section 1414(d)(1)(A)(i)(VIII)

Transition services are linked to outcomes and begin at age 16.

Definition: Section 1401(34) defines "transition services" to be "a coordinated set of activities for a child with a disability that:

1. is "designed to be within a results-oriented process" and is focused on "improving" the student's "academic and functional achievement" in order "to facilitate the (student's) movement from school to post-school activities, including post-secondary education, vocational education, integrated employment (including supported employment), continuing adult education, adult services, independent living, or community participation;"

2. is based on the individual student's needs, taking into account the student's strengths, preferences and interests, and

3. includes instruction, related services, community

experiences, the development of employment, and other post-school adult living objectives, and, when appropriate, acquisition of daily living skills and functional vocational evaluation.

◆ *Significance of Various Terms*
The word "coordinated" means that the services are in sync with each other; there must be more than one service and each service must dovetail with the others. The outcomes are specified (e.g., post-secondary education); employment is preferred to supported employment as indicated by the fact that "supported employment" is in parentheses, and because employment itself is a means for economic self-sufficiency and independent living. Furthermore, the outcomes are "generic" in many respects–the same outcomes as students without disabilities usually are prepared to attain. The transition activities must be based on the student's preferences and thus the student's curriculum should include self-determination instruction and skill-development. The transition curriculum must be community-based and community-referenced, as indicated by the third subsection. The ends or goals are thus connected to the means or curriculum and the transition training is delivered where transition skills are needed (in the community), thus assuring generalizability and durability of skills. Because transition planning is part of the IEP, it must benefit the student; otherwise, it is not appropriate because it will fail the *Rowley* test of benefit. Districts will also be held more accountable for their transition planning as seen with the new phrase "results-oriented." The 2004 amendments specifically add that "As the graduation rates for children with disabilities continue to climb, providing effective transition services to promote successful post-school employment or education is an important measure of accountability for children with disabilities." Section 1400(c)(14).

Transition as Part of IEP, Section 1414(d)(1)(A)(i)(VIII): A student's transition plan is part of the student's IEP. Beginning no later than the first IEP to be in effect when the child is 16, and updated annually thereafter, the IEP must contain "appropriate measurable post-secondary goals, based upon age appropriate transition assessments related to training, education, employment and where appropriate, independent living skills; and "the transition services (including courses of study) needed to assist the child in reaching those goals."

◆ *Significance of Change of Age*
The 2004 amendments have raised the age for transition planning from 14 to 16, and specified that transition planning should be related to training, education, employment, and independent living skills. This directly reflects the IDEA policy outcomes of "helping children with disabilities achieve equality of opportunity, full participation, independent living and economic self-sufficiency" and preparing them to lead "productive and independent lives." Section 1400(c)(1) and Section 1400 (c)(5)(A).

Age of Majority and Transfer of Rights, Section 1414(d)(1)(A)(i)(VIII): Beginning no later than one year before the student reaches the age of majority under state law, the IEP must contain a statement that the student has been informed of the student's rights under IDEA, if any, that will transfer to the student when he or she reaches the age of majority.

◆ *Significance*
These subsections are the "devolution" provisions; they provide that the rights of the student's parents will devolve to the student when the student achieves the age of majority (usually, 18). They advance the concept of competency of the student (competent by reason of age and capacity to make decisions and participate in shared educational decision-making).

XV. Tuition Reimbursement as Remedy for Denying Appropriate Education

In *School Committee of the Town of Burlington v. Department of Education of Massachusetts,* 471 U.S. 359 (1985), the Supreme Court held that IDEA requires LEAs to reimburse parents for their expenditures for private placement if the LEA does not provide the student an educational benefit but the private school does. The Court based its decision on two factors: a) the LEA does not provide an appropriate education, but b) the private school was able to provide an appropriate education.

The 2004 amendments codify the Court's decision but add exceptions and limitations.

General Rule: Section 1412(a)(10)(C)(i) does not require an LEA to pay for the cost of the student's education, including special education and related services, at a private school or facility if the LEA made a free appropriate public education available to the student and the student's parents instead elected to place their child in the private school or facility instead.

◆ Significance of the General Rule
The basic rule of IDEA is that the federal funds will be used for public education; thus "free appropriate public education" (FAPE) is the overall principle of IDEA. When a parent chooses private education over public education, the parent also chooses to pay for that education and not to charge the tuition to the LEA. We explained the consequences of the parents' choice under Zero Reject, "Comprehensive Coverage."

Exception: Section 1412(a)(10)(C)(ii) codifies the Court's rule, an exception to the "public" in FAPE: "If the parents of a child with a disability, who previously received special education and related services under the authority of a public agency, enroll the child in a private elementary school or secondary school without the consent of or referral by the public agency, a court or a hearing officer may require the agency to reimburse the parents for the cost of that enrollment if the court or hearing officer finds that the agency had not made a free appropriate public education available to the child in a timely manner prior to that enrollment."

◆ Significance of the Exception
If a hearing officer finds that the LEA failed to offer an appropriate education, the officer may charge the tuition to the LEA because the LEA defaulted in its obligation and the parent elected the private school as a way to secure the right to an appropriate education.

Limitations: Section 1412(a)(10)(C)(iii) limits the amount of reimbursement based on parents' action or inaction. Most of the limitations were determined by various courts before the 2004 amendments and now have been codified: Thus, the cost of reimbursement may be reduced or denied–

1. if–

   a. at the "most recent" IEP meeting the parents attended before removing their child from the LEA ("public school"), they did not inform the IEP team that they were rejecting the "placement proposed" by the LEA to provide FAPE and also did not "stat(e) their concerns and their intent to enroll their child in a private school at public expense"; or

b. "10 business days (including any holidays that occur on a business day)" before removing their child from the public school, the parents did not give written notice to the "public agency" that they were rejecting the IEP;

2. "if, before the removal, the "public agency" informed the parents (through the notice requirements described in Section 1415(b)(3)), that it intends to evaluate the student (including a statement of the purpose of the evaluation that was appropriate and reasonable), but the parents did not make their child available for that evaluation; or

3. "upon judicial finding of unreasonableness with respect to actions taken by the parents."

◆ *Significance of Notice and Response*

These provisions are the essence of fairness. They require the parents to notify the LEA so the LEA may "cure" any default in appropriate education and thus avoid tuition reimbursement. Note especially that the 2004 amendments (a) require parents to say why they are disenrolling their child; (b) give the LEA an opportunity to evaluate the child so that it may address the parents' concerns; (c) require the LEA to make an "appropriate and reasonable" statement why it wants to evaluate the child; and (d) allow for denial or reduction of tuition reimbursement if the parents do not allow the LEA to evaluate their child. Thus, this section compels parents and LEA to confront the issue of an inappropriate education and to try to develop one. That is why this section allows a "judicial" (court ordered–but perhaps includes order by a hearing officer) determination that the parents acted unreasonably; they must be reasonable or risk forfeiting their claim to tuition reimbursement.

Reimbursement Not Reduced, Denied, Section 1412(a)(10)(C)(iv)(I): The cost of reimbursement shall not be reduced or denied if (a) the LEA prevented the parent from providing the required notice; (b) the parents had not received notice that they had to notify the LEA of their intentions to seek reimbursement; or (c) compliance with the no-reimbursement without parental notice rule "would likely result in physical harm to the child."

◆ *Significance of Three Defenses Against Reduction*
These three defenses also reflect a fairness approach. School malfeasance or negligence are excuses to the parental notice requirement, as is danger of physical harm to the child. Note that these categories are now a definite "shall not" as opposed to a "may" reason for not reducing or denying reimbursement.

Reimbursement "May" be Reduced, Denied, Section 1412(a)(10)(C) (iv)(II): The cost of reimbursement may not, in the discretion of a court or a hearing officer, be reduced or denied if the parent failed to give the required notice because the parent is illiterate and cannot write in English or if compliance with the parental notice rule "would likely result in serious emotional harm to the child."

◆ *Significance*
The 2004 amendments separate two categories where reimbursement "may" be reduced or denied for failure to give parental notice: illiteracy and emotional harm (as distinguished from physical harm) to the child. This decision now rests with either a court or hearing officer.

XVI. Additional Remedies: Extended School Year Services (ESY) and Compensatory Education

ESY: Extended school year services (ESY) are available to students who may regress or experience significant delays in recouping their progress because they are out of school during the summer. IDEA, as interpreted by many courts, entitles students to receive an appropriate education during summers and/or other periods when the LEA ceases services for its students. The students' IEPs should provide for ESY services. ESY also is an "equitable" remedy (one that is in a court's discretion) that can be imposed by the court in response to a violation of FAPE. The right to an appropriate education demands individualized education regardless of the predetermined number of school days in any given district.

Compensatory Education: Still another remedy is education over and above that to which the student otherwise would be entitled, typically, beyond the student's 21st birthday or expected graduation date. Compensatory education is available as an equitable remedy. Compensatory education is awardable when the LEA denies the student a "basic floor of opportunity" as is the student's right under *Rowley*. The court will consider the length of time that the LEA refused to confer an educational benefit and the consequences of that denial. Both considerations must be "gross" or "flagrant."

While these remedies are not specifically written into IDEA, they are consistent with and rest on the Supreme Court's tuition-reimbursement decision in *Burlington* and, under the theory of individualized access to a basic floor of opportunity, provide additional avenues through which students may receive services if the LEA fails to provide an appropriate education.

XVII. Early Intervention for Infants and Toddlers and Their Families Provisions, Part C, Sections 1431-1445

Part C services are outcome/result- oriented, their purposes (Section 1431(a)) being to:

1. enhance a child's development, minimize the potential for developmental delay, and recognize the significant brain development that occurs during a child's first 3 years of life;

2. reduce educational costs by minimizing the need for special education and related services after infants and toddlers with disabilities reach school age;

3. maximize the potential for individuals with disabilities to live independently in society;

4. enhance families' capacity to meet the special needs of their infants and toddlers with disabilities; and

5. enhance the capacity of state and local agencies and service providers to identify, evaluate, and meet the needs of all children, particularly minority, low-income, inner-city, and rural children, and infants and toddlers in foster care. Section 1431(a).

◆ Significance of Outcome-Oriented Policy for Infants, Families, and Providers

Early intervention has always been outcome-oriented, with the five outcomes being concerned with the child, the family, and the service system. As much if not more than any other declaration of federal policy, Section 1431 proclaims that the nation's goals are to preserve and strengthen the families of children with disabilities and the children themselves, while, at the same time, developing state and local capacities to serve them. This "dual accommodation" approach—focused on the family and child on the one hand and the system on the other—now characterizes Part B of IDEA (ages 3-21).

◆ Significance of Special-Needs Population and Brain Research

Just as NCLB and Part B of IDEA focus on the needs of minority and other members of the IDEA beneficiary class, so too does Part C. Here we see Congress' effort to use special education as a preventive intervention. That is especially so by reason of the reference to brain research; the reference mirrors the "scientifically/evidence-based" approach that both NCLB and IDEA require.

XVIII. Nature of Early Intervention Services, Section 1432(4)

There are 14 different early intervention services, some focused exclusively on the child and some on the family, though all benefit both the child and the family. The services are provided under public supervision, at no cost to the family (unless federal or state law provide for fee-charging, including sliding fees), meet state standards, and target the child's physical, cognitive, communication, social or emotional, and adaptive development.

◆ Significance

By targeting these five domains of the child's development, this section prepares the child to participate in the general curriculum, beginning at age 3, under NCLB and IDEA.

XIX. Individualized Family Service Plan (IFSP), Section 1436

The plan for infants and toddlers is similar to the IEP for students ages 3-21. It must be in writing, and contain:

1. a statement of the child's present levels of physical development, cognitive development, communication development, social or emotional development, and adaptive development, based on objective criteria

◆ *Significance*
Now, the IEP is like the IFSP, in that it is "domain-based" and rests on objective evaluation data.

2. a statement of the family's resources, priorities, and concerns relating to enhancing the child's development

◆ *Significance*
Here, the family itself becomes the beneficiary of the services; it joins the child as a co-beneficiary. Some of the related services available to children ages 3-21 also benefit families, such as school social work, psychological services, and counseling services. Increasingly, schools are expected to benefit the child and the family alike. That expectation is part of the trend toward service-integration and requires family-centered, culturally responsive services.

3. a statement of the measurable results or outcomes expected to be achieved for the child and family, including pre-literacy and language skills, as developmentally appropriate for the child; the criteria, procedures, and timelines used to determine the degree to which progress toward achieving the results or outcomes is being made; and whether modifications or revisions of the results or outcomes or services are necessary

◆ *Significance of "Language and Literacy" Rule*
The 2004 amendments have added pre-language and literacy skills to this subsection, thus making it a precursor to the reading-based services for students ages 3 to 21 under Part B and also mirroring NCLB's emphasis on having students be proficient in reading. Like the IEP, this provision assures accountability for outcomes.

4. a statement of specific early intervention services based on peer-reviewed research, to the extent practicable, necessary

to meet the child's and family's unique needs, including the frequency, intensity, and method of delivering services

◆ Significance

This provision re-emphasizes that the interventions must be scientifically based, consistent with NCLB and IDEA Part B.

5. a statement of the natural environments in which early intervention services shall appropriately be provided, including a justification of the extent, if any, to which the services will not be provided in a natural environment

◆ Significance

This is the "least restrictive environment" provision as applied to infants and toddlers.

6. the projected dates for initiating the services and the anticipated length, duration, and frequency of the services

7. identification of the service coordinator from the profession most immediately relevant to the child's or family's needs (or who is otherwise qualified to carry out all applicable responsibilities) who will be responsible for implementing the plan and coordinating with other agencies and persons, including transition services

◆ Significance

This provision parallels the NCLB and IDEA provisions about "highly qualified" professionals because it requires the service coordinator to be from an appropriate profession or be otherwise qualified. There is also an addition that the service coordinator must be responsible for "transition." This provision complements the provisions about transition planning and the parent's right to invite the coordinator to an initial IEP meeting.

8. the steps to be taken to support the child's transition to preschool or other appropriate services.

◆ Significance

Transition is also assisted because the child's IFSP may be the IEP if the parents and LEA consent. Section 1414(d)(2)(B).

XX. IFSP Team, Section 1436

The IFSP team is a multidisciplinary team comprised of the child's parents and other qualified personnel. Parents are entitled to have the IFSP "fully explained" and must give or withhold "written consent" before the child receives any of the services that the plan describes. If the parents do not provide consent with respect to a particular early intervention service, then only the early intervention services to which consent is obtained shall be provided.

◆ *Significance of Membership*
Section 1436 is silent about whether parents may bring chosen professionals or advocates to the meeting to develop the IFSP. Further, although Section 1436 does not identify any professional members of the IFSP team, clearly it anticipates that they will represent the various disciplines necessary to achieve the child and family outcomes set out in Section 1431 and the services enumerated in Section 1432. Note that the parents may consent to some services and withhold consent to others, consistent with IDEA's and NCLB's Parent Participation Principle; they may basically "cherry pick" the services in early intervention, unlike in Part B or in general education. Here, the parents are put into the IFSP process, that is, into the decision-making process related to the child's development, from the outset. Parents will be able to rely on their IFSP experience when their child becomes eligible for an IEP; their collaboration and advocacy skills will have been honed during the IFSP process. Also, the necessary experts that need to be included in the IFSP development are identified and put into the decision-making process, as in the IEP.

XXI. Contents of the IFSP, Section 1436(a), include:

1. a multidisciplinary assessment of the child's unique

    strengths and needs and the identification of services appropriate to meet such needs

◆ *Significance*
The assessment must be non-discriminatory, consistent with IDEA Part B and Section 504.

2. a family-directed assessment of the family's resources, priorities, and concerns and the identification of the supports and services necessary to enhance the family's capacity to meet their child's developmental needs

◆ *Significance*
"Family-directed" is appropriate when the beneficiary of the services is the family, as this provision directs. Moreover, "family-centered" service-provision is also appropriate.

3. a written individualized family service plan developed by a multidisciplinary team, including the parents, including a description of the appropriate transition services for the child toddler.

◆ *Significance*
Here, again, the family is a decision-maker, services are family-centered, and the child's and family's transition to early childhood education (age 3 and above) is planned.

XXII. Timing, Section 1436(b) and (c)

The IFSP must be developed "within a reasonable period of time" after the child's "assessment" is "complete." The IFSP must be evaluated at least once a year and the family has the right to a review the plan at 6-month intervals or more often where appropriate based on infant or toddler and family needs, Section 1436(b). With the parents' consent, early intervention services may commence before the assessment is complete, Section 1436(c).

◆ *Significance*
Earlier services are better, even when the full assessment is incomplete; and frequent review is better in light of the usually fast-changing needs of infants and their families.

Least Restrictive Environment:
The Fourth of the Six Principles

I. Reviewing the Six Principles and Introducing the Presumption Favoring Inclusion

Originally known as "mainstreaming" and now sometimes referred to as "integration" or "inclusion," this principle has the potential for significantly improving students' education; redressing their exclusion from educational opportunities and post-school access; contributing to the education of all pupils; encouraging the training of all educators; and enlightening the public at large about the nature of disability and about students with disabilities. The 2004 amendments build on the first three principles; enhance the LRE rule; and continue to presume that a student will participate in the academic, extracurricular, and other non-academic programs of the LEA. IDEA specifically states that the education of children with disabilities can be made more effective by:

> "having high expectations for such children and ensuring their access to the general education curriculum in the regular classroom, to the maximum extent possible, in order to meet developmental goals and, to the maximum extent possible, the challenging expectations that have been established for all children; and be prepared to lead productive and independent adult lives, to the maximum extent possible..." Section 1400(c)(5).

The IDEA thus enacts a presumption that students with disabilities will be granted access to and educated in the general education curriculum and will participate in other general education activities. This presumption in favor of inclusion in, and progress through, the general education curriculum has always been part of IDEA.

By using IDEA's Principles of Zero Reject, Non-Discriminatory Evaluation, and Appropriate Education and the IDEA provisions that effectuate these principles, the 2004 amendments grant students access to the general education curriculum so that they can make progress under IDEA and as measured against the high standards for "all children" under NCLB. Children with disabilities now will be expected to receive the accommodations and adjustments necessary to participate in local and state assessments under NCLB.

Note, however, that the LRE presumption is a rebuttable presumption. Although the presumption is in favor of an LRE placement (that is, integration or inclusion) "to the maximum extent appropriate," the term "appropriate" is defined in relation to each student's individual needs. If LRE (integration or inclusion) is not appropriate for a given student in the *Rowley* sense of opportunity to benefit, then the presumption may be rebutted.

Moreover, the LRE rule promotes three public policy values: (a) the value of an appropriate education for students with disabilities; (b) the value of having students with and without disabilities associate with each other, thus removing the stigma of "difference/disability"; and (c) the value of conservation of fiscal capital, it usually being less expensive to operate one school system than two segregated ones.

II. The General Rule, Section 1412(a)(5)

The general rule of LRE is set out in Section 1412(a)(5): "To the maximum extent appropriate, students with disabilities...[will be] educated with students who are not disabled, and special classes, separate schooling or other removal of students with disabilities from the regular educational environment [may occur] only when the nature or severity of the disability of a child is such that education in regular classes with the use of supplementary aids and services cannot be achieved satisfactorily for that student."

◆ *Significance*
The presumption is set out here: Include unless not appropriate.

III. Strengthening the Presumption, "Extent, If Any," Section 1414(d)(1)(A)(i)(V)

This section strengthens the presumption by requiring the student's IEP to contain "an explanation of the extent, if any, to which the child will not participate" with non-disabled children in the regular class and in "the general education curriculum" and "extracurricular and other non-academic activities."

◆ *Significance of the Three Dimensions of "LRE"*
IDEA requires the IEP team to justify any removal from the least restrictive environment and defines the three dimensions of that environment and thus of the term "regular education" or "general education": the general education curriculum, extracurricular activities, and other school activities such as recess, meal-times, transportation, dances, or spectator-sport activities.

◆ *Significance of the "If Any" Language–Justification and "Mix and Match" Approach*
This section also requires the IEP team to explain "the extent, if any," to which the student will be segregated; thus, it allows for partial inclusion where total inclusion is not appropriate. It also puts the burden of proof on the LEA to justify any partial or total exclusion, not merely to explain the extent of exclusion. Further, the IEP team must consider each dimension listed above and the extent to which the student must be removed for an appropriate education. This provision allows for "mix and match" where total integration is appropriate under one dimension and partial integration is appropriate under another dimension.

IV. Securing Access to the LRE/General Curriculum Via NDE and AE

As we have noted in Part Two: Non-Discriminatory Evaluation, and Part Three: Appropriate Education, IDEA links evaluation, appropriate education/IEP, and LRE to create a seamless approach to educating the student.

Accordingly, the non-discriminatory evaluation/individualized education program team must evaluate the student and focus especially on developing a program that leads to placement in the general education curriculum. Section 1414(b)(2)(A).

Moreover, a student may not be classified into special education where the "determinant factor" for potential special education classification involves the "lack of appropriate instruction in reading, including the essential components of reading instruction (as defined in section 1208(3) of the Elementary and Secondary

Act of 1965), lack of instruction in math, or limited English proficiency." Section 1414(b)(5).

◆ *Significance of Link and Limitation*

By requiring the NDE/IEP team to link evaluation and program to placement, and by disqualifying a student from special education under IDEA (but not necessarily from "reasonable accommodations" under Section 504 and ADA), Sections 1414(b)(2) and (5) attempt to ensure that only those students who "need" special education are placed there. If those students do not "need" special education, they must remain in general education. The term "need" derives directly from the IDEA definition of "child with a disability" in Section 1401(3).

Moreover, the NDE/IEP team must use "a variety of assessment tools and strategies" that "may assist" the team in acquiring "information related to enabling the child to be involved in and progress in the general education curriculum or, for preschool children, to participate in appropriate activities," Section 1414(b)(2)(A).

In addition, when conducting an initial evaluation or a reevaluation, the team must determine "whether any additions to or modifications to the special education and related services are needed to enable the child to...participate, as appropriate, in the general education curriculum." Section 1414(c)(1)(B)(iv).

Next, as we pointed out in Part Three: Non-Discriminatory Evaluation, the student's IEP must contain

  a. a statement of "how the child's disability affects the child's involvement in and progress in the general curriculum," Section 1414(d)(1)(A)(i)(I);

  b. measurable annual goals, "including academic and functional goals, designed to meet the child's needs to enable the child to be involved in and make progress in the general education curriculum," Section 1414(d)(1)(A) (i)(II);

  c. a statement of related services and supplementary aids and services and "a statement of the program modifications or supports for school personnel that will be provided for the child...to be involved in and make

69

progress in the general education curriculum...and to participate in extracurricular and other nonacademic activities," Section 1414(d)(1)(A)(i) (IV); and

d. a statement regarding state and district-wide assessments and what accommodations are necessary to measure the academic and functional performance of the child consistent with NCLB, whether the student will participate in them, and, if the student is not to participate in them, why and what other assessments the student will undergo, Section 1414(d)(1)(A)(i) (VI).

◆ *Significance of Content Requirements*
These provisions about IEP content implement the LRE presumption. They make clear that exclusion from the general curriculum is the exception, not the rule.

The individualized education program team must include a general educator, Section 1414(d)(1)(B)(ii). That person has specific duties relating to the student's participation in the general curriculum, namely, to identify the program modifications and supports that advance the LRE placement, Section 1414(d)(3)(C). The team must also include an LEA representative who is "knowledgeable about the general curriculum and...about the availability of resources" of the LEA that can be brought to bear on appropriate education in the least restrictive environment, Section 1414(d)(1)(B)(iv).

Finally, as we noted in Part Three: AE, Appropriate Education, and particularly under "transition," the transition components of a student's IEP focus on "full participation" outcomes (Section 1401(34)(A)) and their implementation through inclusive methods such as community service, employment and other post-school objectives, Section 1401(34)(C).

◆ *Significance Overall*
IDEA defines the general curriculum (academic, extracurricular, and other school activities) and links the student's placement in the general curriculum to the non-discriminatory evaluation and the individualized education program. Provisions related to the team membership also advance the LRE rule; they require a general educator and a person knowledgeable about resources that can be used to achieve an LRE placement. Last, the

transition provisions tie to the student's post-school life in the least restrictive environment that non-disabled adults enjoy.

Procedural Due Process:
The Fifth of the Six Principles

I. Reviewing the Six Principles and the Nature of Procedural Due Process

The first four principles (Zero Reject, Non-Discriminatory Evaluation, Appropriate Education, and Least Restrictive Environment) constitute "in-puts" to a student's education. They are what SEAs and LEAs do for the student.

They also encapsulate the rights that the students and their parents have and may enforce against the SEAs and LEAs that do not comply with IDEA. Rights without remedies, however, are meaningless. So IDEA confers rights on the students and parents to enforce their IDEA rights. Further, IDEA recognizes that SEAs and LEAs also have rights, so it confers on those agencies various rights against students and parents. In short, the Principle of Procedural Due Process is a mutual-enforcement principle.

In a larger sense, however, the principle proclaims that SEAs, LEAs, students, and parents should deal fairly with each other, and it sets out the procedures for fair dealing. As Justice Felix Frankfurter once wrote, fairness is the essence of due process (*Anti-Fascist Committee v. McGrath*, 341 U.S. 123 (1951)).

II. Procedural Due Process in General, Section 1415

Due process consists of the right to protest actions of parents, the SEA, or the LEA through mediation, appeal to an impartial hearing officer, and appeal to state or federal courts.

◆ *Significance*
The 2004 amendments continue IDEA's prior protections, including notice, access to records, parent participation and due process hearings. However, Section 1400(c)(8) adds a finding that "parents and schools should have expanded opportunities to resolve their disagreements in positive and constructive ways."

Thus, Section 1415 shifts the emphasis from due process hearings to alternative means such as mediation and a newly imposed mandatory resolution session. There also are new, more stringent notice and complaint requirements and an opportunity for parents or the LEA to claim that the due process complaint notice is insufficient.

◆ *Significance*

Under the 2004 amendments, the 30 days preceding a due process hearing have become, essentially, a due process hearing without the actual due process hearing; these 30 days take the function of a hearing without the formality of one.

First, the party requesting due process has to file a complaint that describes the problem related to the student, the facts of that problem, and a proposed resolution to the problem.

Next, the party responding to the complaint has the opportunity to challenge the sufficiency of this notice (a factual issue).

This action is followed by the hearing officer making a ruling essentially on the sufficiency of the complaint. If the notice is found to be not sufficient, the party requesting due process must give more factual details.

Then, the issues are set out in a face-to-face discussion at the mandatory resolution session.

Through all of this, the responding party has the opportunity to cure the factual issues in the complaint by having total access to information that forms the basis of the complaint, long before the parties have to exchange information five days before the hearing.

III. Parental Consent, Section 1414(c)(3)

Consent for Evaluation: An LEA must obtain consent from a student's parents to conduct the initial and all subsequent evaluations. As we noted under Non-Discriminatory Evaluation, the LEA may go to mediation or due process if the parents refuse consent for an initial evaluation. Section 1414(a)(1)(D). In the case of reevaluations, the LEA may conduct the reevaluation if they have taken "reasonable" steps to secure parental consent but have been unable to do so. Section 1414(c)(3).

Absence of Consent: The parents' failure to consent or refusal to consent may be overruled only after a due process hearing (or appeal) where hearing officer finds in favor of the LEA. Section 1414 (a)(1)(D)(ii).

Limitation on Scope of Consent: A consent for evaluation does not commit a parent to consenting to special education or related services for the child. Section 1414 (a)(1)(D)(i)(I). Rather, the LEA must seek "informed consent" from the parent before initiating services. Section 1414 (a)(1)(D)(i)(II).

LEA Absolved if No Consent (Refusal to Give Consent): If a parent does not consent to services after evaluation, the LEA is not to "provide special education and related services to the child by utilizing the [due process] procedures in Section 1415." Section 1414(a)(1)(D) (ii)(II). Under those circumstances, the LEA is absolved from any obligations to provide FAPE or develop an IEP for that child. Section 1414(a)(1)(D)(ii)(III).

Consent Defined: "Consent" as defined in Sec. 300.500 of the 1999 IDEA regulations means that the parents have been fully informed, in their native language or in another suitable method of communication, of all the information relevant to the activity for which the LEA seeks consent, that the parents understand and agree in writing that the activity may be carried out, that the request for consent describes the activity and lists all records released and to whom, and that the parents understand that their consent is voluntary and may be revoked at any time.

◆ *Significance in General*
Parents have a legal and moral duty to their child; this duty requires them to assure that their child is educated (hence, the truancy laws are enforceable against parents). Parents also have a legal right to consent or not consent to educational, medical, or similar procedures to which their child will be subjected. IDEA codifies these general rights and at the same time seeks to create, through parental consent, a means whereby parents and educators will be partners with each other and share the decision-making that affects a child's education.

◆ *Significance of Refusal to Consent and Absolution*
A parent who refuses to give consent to services after evaluation surrenders the student's rights to IDEA. The parent may not later complain that the LEA failed to provide the student with FAPE at a later date.

Surrogate Parents: The SEA may assign surrogate parents where the child's parents are unknown or unavailable. Section 1415(b)(2).

IV. General Notice Requirements, Section 1415(b)(3), Section 1415(c)

General Notice (also known as a Notice of Action): An SEA or LEA must give prior written notice to parents, guardians, or surrogate parents whenever it "proposes to initiate a change; or refuses to initiate or change the identification, evaluation, or educational placement of the child or the provision of a free appropriate public education to the child." Section 1415(b)(3).

◆ *Significance*
This section refers to the notice that the SEA or LEA must give whenever it wants to act or refuses to act. This is a general notice.

Contents of General Notice, Section 1415(c): The general notice must include:

1. a description of the action that the SEA or LEA proposes or refuses to take;

2. the agency's explanation why it proposes or refuses to take the action and a description of each evaluation procedure, assessment, record, or report that the agency used as a basis for the proposed or refused action;

3. a statement that the parents have certain protections under the procedural safeguards, and, if this notice is not an initial referral for evaluation, how the parents may obtain a copy of a description of the procedural safeguards can be obtained;

4. the sources that parents can contact to obtain assistance in understanding the provisions in the notice;

5. a description of any other options considered by the IEP team and the reason why those options were rejected; and

6. a description of other factors that are relevant to the agency's proposal or refusal.

◆ *Significance*

This section requires the SEA or LEA to justify its action and inform the parents what steps they may take if they disagree with the agency's proposed action, thereby putting them at a more "even table" with the LEA.

V. Procedural Safeguards Notice, Section 1415(d)(1)(A)

In addition to the general notice, IDEA provides for a "procedural safeguards notice" whenever an SEA or LEA takes or proposes to take certain action. This is a second notice that supplements the first, general notice.

General Rule: As a general rule, the LEA must give the procedural safeguards notice to the parents only one time each year (presumably, "school year").

Exceptions: The exceptions to the once-a-year notice are as follows:

1. when the student is referred for the initial referral or when the parents request an evaluation;

2. when the parents or agency file the first complaint under subsection 1415(b)(6); and

3. upon request by a parent.

Internet Posting, Section 1415(d)(1)(B): An LEA may place a current copy of the procedural safeguards notice on its Internet website if it has a website.

Content of Notice, Section 1415(d)(2): The procedural safeguards notice must include a full explanation of the procedural safeguards, written in the parents' native language (unless it clearly is not feasible to do so), and written in an easily understandable manner, relating to–

1. independent educational evaluation (see also Section 1415(b)(1))

2. prior written notice

3. parental consent

4. access to educational records

5. the opportunity to present and resolve complaints, including the time period in which to make a complaint; the opportunity for the agency to resolve the complaint; and the availability of mediation

6. the child's placement during the pendency of due process proceedings

7. procedures for students who are subject to placement in an interim alternative educational setting

8. requirements for unilateral placement by parents of children in private schools at public expense

9. due process hearings, including requirements for disclosure of evaluation results and recommendations

10. state-level appeals (if applicable in that state)

11. civil actions, included the time period in which to file such actions

12. attorneys' fees.

◆ *Significance*

The frequency of the procedural safeguards notice requirements has been amended to reduce the paperwork burden that SEAs and LEAs have complained about. As a trade-off, however, the 2004 amendments require even more specific information than previously, and the information relates essentially to all of the child's IDEA rights and how the parents can enforce those rights. Congress clearly intends that there will be no uninformed parents and that the SEA and LEA will make a full disclosure of IDEA rights.

VI. Complaints (Requests for Due Process Hearings), Section 1415(b)(6)

If fairness is the essence of due process, then fairness can exist only if the parents and the SEA, LEA, or other public agency are treated nearly, if not exactly, equally. The 2004 amendments try to be fair to the agencies and parents alike.

Who May File a Complaint, Section 1415(b)(6): The 2004 amendments now allow parents, the SEA, LEA, or any other interested party to file a complaint with respect to any matter relating to the identification, evaluation, educational placement of the child, or the provision of a free appropriate public education to such child. Note that if a parent refuses to allow the student into special education, the parent loses any right to complain under IDEA about the student's education.

Content of Complaint, Section 1415(b)(6)(B): The complaint must set forth an alleged violation that occurred not more than two years before the date the parents or the public agency knew or should have known about the action that allegedly forms the basis of the complaint, or, if the state has an explicit time limitation for presenting such a complaint under this part, then, as a general rule, within such time as the state law allows. There are exceptions to this general rule.

◆ *Significance of Notice*
The notice requirement prevents parents, the LEA, or other parties from catching the opposing party unawares. It thereby allows the party receiving the complaint to "cure" or attempt to cure any problems that were identified and also to know (in advance of mediation or a due process hearing) exactly the nature of the complaint and what remedies are being sought.

Two-Year Statute of Limitations: The 2004 amendments add a statute of limitations provision. A "statute of limitations" is a rule of law that prohibits a party from bringing a complaint or other legal action against another party for an alleged violation of the law after a specified amount of time. Here, the violation of IDEA may not have occurred more than two years before the party files the complaint.

Complaint and Due Process Notice Given Simultaneously, Section 1415(b)(7)(A): When a complaint is filed, the party, or the attorney representing a party, must provide a due process complaint notice ("which shall remain confidential") to the other party and forward a copy to the SEA. The notice must contain the following:

1. the student's name and residence address and the name of the school the student is attending

2. in the case of a homeless child or youth (within the meaning of section 725(2) of the McKinney-Vento Homeless Assistance Act (42 U.S.C. 11434a(2)), available contact information for the student and the name of the school the student is attending

3. a description of the "nature of the problem of the child relating to (the) proposed initiation or change, including facts relating to (the) problem"

4. a proposed resolution of the problem to the extent known and available to the party at the time.

No Hearing Without Complaint, Section 1415(b)(7)(B): No party–either the party making the complaint or the party responding to the complaint–may have a due process hearing until the party, or the attorney representing the party, files a notice that meets the requirements stated above.

Sufficiency of Notice, Section 1415(c): The 2004 amendments add several requirements for the due process complaint notice described in Section 1415(c)(1). Generally, the due process complaint shall be deemed "sufficient" unless the party receiving the notice notifies the hearing officer and the notifying party that the receiving party believes that the notice does not meet the requirements of Section 1415(b)(7)(A). This notification must be received by the hearing officer within 15 days of the party receiving the complaint. Then, the hearing officer has to make a decision five days after receiving the notification whether the notice meets the requirements of Section 1415(b)(7), and the hearing officer must notify the parties in writing immediately after making a decision.

Since 1997, a common complaint by LEAs has been that parental requests for due process are too general and do not provide any constructive information that would allow the LEA to remedy the problem. The new "sufficiency" requirement allows the complaint to be weighed as to its factual content long before due process, and starts a discovery process in which the parties will present all of the relevant issues in a paperwork exchange.

LEA Response to Parent Complaint, Section 1415(c)(2) (B)(i)(I): If the LEA is the party receiving the parents' notice of a violation (a complaint), and if the LEA has not sent a prior written notice to the parents about the issue contained in the complaint (see Section 1415(c)(1)), the LEA must send a response within 10 days that describes

1. the action that the LEA proposed or refused

2. any other options considered by the IEP team and the reason why the team rejected those options were rejected

3. each evaluation procedure, assessment, record, or report that the LEA used as a basis for its proposed or refused action

4. other factors that are relevant to the LEA's proposal or refusal.

Even if the LEA responds by sending out this notice, the LEA may still assert (within 15 days) that the parents' notice was insufficient. Section 1415(c)(2) (B)(i)(II).

◆ *Significance*
The LEA may challenge the sufficiency of the parents' notice while also defending the allegations on substantive grounds. Otherwise, the party who receives the complaint has 10 days to send a response that specifically addresses the issues raised in the complaint. Section 1415(c)(2) (B)(ii).

Amending the Complaint, Section 1415(c)(2)(E): The complaint may be amended only if the other party consents, in writing, and is given the opportunity to resolve the complaint through the resolution session, or, if the hearing officer grants permission to amend, not later than five days before due process is scheduled to begin.

◆ *Significance*

This provision requires the complainant to set out, at the very beginning of the dispute, every alleged violation. It may forestall repeated amendments that protract a resolution of the complaint. But it also puts a heavy burden on the complainant to know exactly all of the violations and to allege them specifically.

VII. Mediation: Section 1415(e)

The SEA must "allow" parties to disputes "involving any matter, including matters arising prior to the filing of a complaint...to resolve such disputes through a mediation process."

◆ *Significance*

Congress continues to recognize that due process hearings and appeals to a court both reflect and exacerbate miscommunication (and perhaps more) between the parents and the SEA or LEA. The 2004 amendments acknowledge the argument that due process hearings are a drain to all parties, both financially and emotionally. The amendments hope to forestall those costs and to preserve collaborative decision-making between the parents and the SEA or LEA, by making mediation a legally binding option. The amendments also clarify that mediation is available before a complaint is filed.

The mediation procedures "shall ensure that the mediation process (a) is voluntary on the part of the parties; (b) is not used to deny or delay a parent's right to a due process hearing...or to deny any other rights" under IDEA, and (c) is conducted by a qualified and impartial mediator who is trained in effective mediation techniques." Section 1415(e)(2)(A).

◆ *Significance*

Mediation may precede a due process hearing but, since justice delayed is justice denied, it must not get in the way of the parents' request for a hearing.

If the parents or the LEA "choose not to use the mediation process," the SEA must have in place a process to offer "an opportunity to meet, at a time and location convenient to the parents, with a disinterested party...to encourage the use, and explain the benefits, of the mediation process," Section 1415(e)(2(B).

◆ *Significance*
The parties may not be compelled to mediate but their decision not to mediate should at least be well informed.

The SEA bears the entire fiscal responsibility for the mediation process. Section 1415(e)(2)(D).

◆ *Significance*
Because neither the LEA nor parents bear any costs associated with mediation, they have no fiscal disincentive to avoid mediation.

The mediation itself must be scheduled "in a timely manner and...held in a location...convenient to the parties." Section 1415(e)(2)(E).

Mediation can result in a written, legally binding agreement if a resolution is met during mediation. This document must set forth all discussions that occurred, with the caveat that these discussions are confidential and may not be used as evidence in any subsequent due process hearing or civil proceedings. The document must be signed by both the parents and the LEA representative and is enforceable in any state court of competent jurisdiction or district court of the United States. Section 1415(e)(2)(F).

◆ *Significance*
The 2004 amendments have made mediation legally binding on the parties, which should increase interest in the process. Otherwise, the language continues to support that mediation should be simple, frank, and non-prejudicial to any hearings; this is the norm for mediation outside of IDEA.

VIII. Resolution Session: Section 1415(f)(1)(B)

The 2004 amendments add a new provision for a "resolution session" as a prerequisite to a due process hearing. This meeting is mandatory unless the parents and the LEA agree in writing to waive the meeting or agree to use the mediation process discussed above.

The LEA has 15 days from receiving notice of the parents' complaint to schedule a meeting with the parents, the relevant members of the IEP team, and a representative of the LEA who has decision-making authority. The LEA attorney is not to be included unless the parents are accompanied by an attorney.

During the resolution session, parents have the opportunity to discuss their complaint and the LEA has the opportunity to resolve the issues. If a resolution is reached, the parties must execute and sign a legally binding agreement that is legally enforceable in any state court of competent jurisdiction or in a district court of the United States. A party may void the agreement within three business days.

If the LEA has not resolved the problem within 30 days from the receipt of the parents' complaint, the due process hearing may occur and the applicable time lines start to commence.

This meeting shall not be considered a meeting convened as a result of an administrative hearing or judicial action, or an administrative hearing or judicial action, so attorneys' fees may not be awarded related to the meeting.

IX. Due Process Hearings: Section 1415(f)

Who May File a Complaint: The 2004 amendments leave intact the heart of procedural due process under IDEA–the due process hearing. However, as we noted above, several provisions have been added to the requirement. Now, both parents and the LEA clearly have a right to an "impartial due process hearing." Section 1415(f)(1).

Five-Day Disclosure Rule: Not less than five days before the hearing, the parents or agency "shall disclose to all other parties all evaluations completed by that date and recommendations based on the offering party's evaluations that the party intends to use at the hearing." Section 1415(f)(2).

Refusal to Disclose: If the parents or agency refuse to make the required disclosure, the hearing officer "may bar (the noncompliant party) from introducing relevant evaluation or recommendation at the hearing without the consent of the other party." Section 1415(f)(2).

◆ *Significance*
This provision, like the notice that the parents and agency must give each other about the complaints they have against each other, prevents surprise by allowing each party to discover the other's evaluation evidence.

Qualifications of a Hearing Officer, Section 1415(f)(3)(A):
The hearing officer must be impartial and may not be "an employee of the State educational agency or the local educational agency involved in the care of the child," or a "person having a personal or professional interest that conflicts with the person's objectivity in the hearing."

◆ *Significance of "Objectivity" Rule*
The "no conflict of interest" provision has always been part of IDEA, but the 2004 amendments add the "objectivity rule." This rule may limit the ability of parents or LEAs to "judge shop"– essentially, select hearing officers who are known to favor one party or the other.

The 2004 amendments also provide that the hearing officer must possess knowledge of the IDEA statute, regulations and federal and state case law; possess the knowledge and ability to conduct hearings in accordance with appropriate, standard legal practice; and possess the knowledge and ability to render and write decisions in accordance with appropriate, standard legal practice. Section 1415(f)(3)(A).

Raising Issues Outside of the Complaint, Section 1415(f)(3)(B):
The 2004 amendments specifically state that the party requesting the due process hearing is not allowed to raise issues at the due process hearing that were not raised in the due process complaint notice. The only exception is if the other party agrees otherwise.

◆ *Significance*
Again, the party making the complaint needs to be well-informed and prepared to detail all of the relevant facts that might arise at the hearing. The effect of this provision is to limit any surprises for

the parties at the hearing so they know exactly the nature of the complaint and what remedies are being sought.

Statute of Limitations, Section 1415(f)(3)(C): In addition to the two-year statute of limitations for filing a complaint (Section 1415(b)(6)(B)), there is also a new two-year statute of limitations regarding requests for a hearing. The two years is calculated from the date at which the parent or the LEA knew or should have known about the alleged action that forms the complaint. Additionally, if state law has explicit time limitations for requesting a hearing, the state law applies.

◆ *Significance*
The statute of limitations means that if a party becomes aware that the child is not receiving FAPE, that party must act within that time to secure any remedy such as tuition reimbursement, compensatory education, or extended school year services.

Decision of Hearing Officer, Section 1415(f)(3)(E): There is also a significant change to the basis for hearing officer decisions. Under the 2004 amendments, the hearing officer must make a decision on substantive grounds based on the determination of whether the child received FAPE. A hearing officer may not base a denial of FAPE solely on procedural inadequacies unless those inadequacies impeded the child's right to an FAPE, significantly impeded the parents' opportunity to participate in the decision-making process regarding the provision of FAPE to their child, or caused a deprivation of educational benefit.

◆ *Significance*
This provision reflects the Congressional concern that hearing officers were making rulings that a school had denied FAPE and that those rulings were based solely on procedural technicalities. These decisions had costly ramifications for school districts, considering that the LEA had to pay for parents' attorney fees. S. Rept. 185 108th Cong., 1st Sess., 39 (2003). The amendment codifies the case law: "no harm, no foul."

Rights at the Hearing, Section 1415(h): The hearing must be held within 30 days after it is requested and in a place and time convenient to the parties. The parents may decide to close the hearing to the public. The parents and agency have the right to "be accompanied and advised by counsel and by individuals with special knowledge or training with respect to the problems of children with disabilities; ... to present evidence and confront, cross-examine, and compel the attendance of witnesses;...to a written, or, at the option of the parents, electronic verbatim record of (the) hearing...(and)...findings of fact and decisions."

X. Discipline, Section 1415(k)

The 2004 amendments have rewritten and reorganized the discipline provisions previously found in Section 1415(k)(1)-(10). The amendments outline when students with disabilities can be disciplined in the same manner as students without disabilities and when and how they must be treated differently.

General Rule–Same Treatment, Section 1415(k)(1)(C) states the general rule that "... disciplinary procedures applicable to children without disabilities may be applied to the child in the same manner and for the same duration in which the procedures would be applied to children without disabilities...."

◆ *Significance of Same Treatment*
As long as the LEA does not discriminate against students with disabilities, it may take actions consistent with school discipline policy in addressing the behavior problems of all students.

Exceptions to Same Treatment, Section 1415(k) provides three exceptions to the general rule.

First, No-Cessation Exception: IDEA requires the SEA and LEA to comply with the "no cessation" provision:

> "A free appropriate public education is available to all children with disabilities residing in the State between the ages of 3 and 21, inclusive, *including children with disabilities who have been suspended or expelled from school*." Section 1412(a)(1)(A)(emphasis added).

◆ *Significance of No Cessation*
This provision is a rule against "cessation" of services. If a student

85

has been suspended or expelled from school, the student is still entitled to IDEA's benefits and the LEA must continue to serve the student despite the suspension or expulsion. This rule addresses Congress' concern about the heightened impact that a loss of educational services can have on a student with a disability. It also codifies *Honig v. Doe,* 484 U.S. 305 (1988), in which the United States Supreme Court held that an LEA may not expel a student if the student's behavior that triggered the discipline was a manifestation of the student's disability. Thus, the LEA must make a "manifestation determination" and then discipline the student according to whether the student's behavior is or is not a manifestation of the student's discipline.

Second, Address-the-Behavior Exception: When the behavior of a student with a disability results in significant disciplinary action, IDEA generally recognizes that the behavior represents a need that should be addressed if it inhibits the ability of the student to receive FAPE.

◆ *Significance of the Address-the-Behavior Exception*
This provision again recognizes the impact that removal from education placement and services can have on students with disabilities and requires a proactive response by the school district to prevent or at least reduce the likelihood of future disciplinary actions.

Third, Manifestation-of-Disability Exception: When the behavior leading to the disciplinary action is a manifestation of the student's disability, schools may NOT apply disciplinary measures in the same manner and duration as with students without disabilities.

◆ *Significance of Manifestation Exception*
The differing treatment required when behavior is a manifestation of a student's disability reflects the fundamental belief that students with disabilities should not treated the same as students without disabilities for behavior that is not entirely within their ability to control or prevent.

XI. Notice of Rights

The LEA must give the student's parents notice, no later than the date the decision to take disciplinary action is made, concerning the rights that they and the student have to appeal a discipline decision. Section 1415 (k)(1)(H). Parents have the right to appeal, and the SEA or LEA must arrange for an expedited hearing. Section 1415(k)(3).

XII. Discipline for Violation of School Code, Section 1415(k)(1)(A)-(F)

When a student with a disability violates the student code of conduct, whether the LEA can use typical disciplinary measures or must apply the differing treatment exceptions depends upon the context of the violation and what disciplinary actions the school proposes to take.

Unique Circumstances: The 2004 amendments have added a provision that allows school personnel to consider "any unique circumstances on a case-by-case basis when determining whether to order a change of placement for a child with a disability who violates a code of student conduct." Section 1415(k)(1)(A).

◆ *Significance of Unique Circumstances*
This provision is a double-edged sword. On the one side, it protects a student against some discipline if there are circumstances unique to the student and the student's behavior, or the infraction that the student committed. Those circumstances could potentially mitigate (soften) the discipline that the SEA otherwise would impose. On the other side, it also allows the SEA to consider circumstances that do not mitigate but instead call for exacerbated discipline.

Short-Term Removals–Not More than 10 Days: Section 1415(k)(1)(B) allows an LEA to remove, for a period of not more than 10 school days, a student who violates a school code to an appropriate interim educational setting, another setting, or suspension, but only if those alternatives may be applied to children without disabilities. When an LEA imposes a removal for not more than 10 school days, it does not need to make a manifestation determination, and it retains discretionary power to determine whether or not to provide services to the student during that time. In other words, none of the exceptions to the "same treatment rule" applies for removals of not more than 10 days.

◆ *Significance of the Less-than-10-Days Provision*
Honig allowed for short-term (10-day) suspensions, a sort of "cooling off" period. This provision creates a 10-day threshold for when procedural due process procedures required for disciplinary "change of placement"–no cessation of services, manifestation determination, behavior planning – must be followed (discussed below under Longer-Term Change of Placement). While this rule is fairly straightforward when the LEA proposes a single suspension for more than 10 days, it is unclear whether the 10 day threshold is reached when the LEA has suspended a student multiple times for a total number of days that exceeds 10 in a school year. In other words, would two suspensions for six days each be considered two short-term removals or would the second six-day removal–because it brought the total number of removal days to 12–trigger the rule for a disciplinary change of placement? Under the regulations promulgated pursuant to the 1997 statute, it was clear that a disciplinary change of placement occurs whenever the removal is for more than 10 consecutive days, or whenever the student is subjected to a series of removals that constitute a pattern (1) because they cumulate to more than 10 days and (2) because of factors related to the length of each removal, the total amount of time that the student is removed, and the proximity of the removals to each other. It is not clear whether the Department of Education will issue regulations for the 2004 amendments that will be similar or identical to the ones for the 1997 law.

Longer-Term Change of Placement: By contrast, the "change of placement for more than 10 days" is the "longer-term" discipline and is governed by a different rule.

> If school personnel seek to order a change in placement that would exceed 10 school days and the behavior that gave rise to the violation of the school code is determined not to be a manifestation of the child's disability pursuant to subparagraph (E), the relevant disciplinary procedures applicable to children without disabilities may be applied to the child in the same manner and for the same duration in which the procedures would be applied to children without disabilities, except as provided in Section 1415(a)(1)

although it may be provided in an interim alternative educational setting. Section 1415(k)(1)(C).

If the LEA determines that the behavior is a manifestation, then the LEA must comply with the "manifestation determination" rules that we describe below.

◆ *Significance of the "Removal for Not More than 10 Days" and the "Changes of Placement for More than 10 Days"*
IDEA distinguishes between a short-term "removal" and a longer-term "change of placement."

As we discussed above, an LEA may "remove" for not more than 10 days and fully invoke the "same treatment" rule; this is the "short-term" removal that the U.S. Supreme Court allowed in *Honig*. But if an LEA attempts to suspend or expel a student for more than 10 days, which is considered a "change of placement" rather than a "removal," all three exceptions to the same treatment rule must be applied: No Cessation, Address Behavior, and Manifestation.

XIII. Application of No-Cessation and Address-the-Behavior Exceptions

The no cessation and address-the-behavior rules are applied automatically once the 10-day threshold is reached.

A child with a disability who is removed from the child's current placement under subparagraph (G) (irrespective of whether the behavior is determined to be a manifestation of the child's disability) or subparagraph (C) shall–

(i) continue to receive educational services, as provided in section 1412(a)(1), so as to enable the child to continue to participate in the general education curriculum, although in another setting, and to progress toward meeting the goals set out in the child's IEP; and

(ii) receive, as appropriate, a functional behavioral assessment, behavioral intervention services and modifications, that are designed to address the behavior violation so that it does not recur. Section 1415(k)(1)(D)

◆ *Significance of No-Cessation and Address-the-Behavior Rules*

This provision assures that services will be provided during the period of removal and that appropriate assessments and services to address behavior, and reduce the likelihood of occurrence, will be provided. This is consistent with the safe-school principles and outcome-based education.

XIV. Application of the Manifestation Exception

The manifestation exception, along with its additional procedural requirements (see below), applies if the discipline is found to be a manifestation. Thus, IDEA requires an inquiry into whether the violation of the school code was a manifestation of the student's disability. This inquiry is known as a Manifestation Determination.

Membership on the Manifestation Determination Team:
Section 1415(k)(1)(E) provides that the determination must be made by "the LEA, the parent, and relevant members of the IEP team (as determined by the parent and the local educational agency)."

◆ *Significance of Membership on the Manifestation Determination Team*

IDEA does not specify who within an LEA must represent the LEA; that is a matter for the LEA to determine. It does, however, say that the student's parent must be a member of the team and that the LEA and parent must determine who on the student's IEP team is "relevant" for the purposes of determining manifestation. That makes sense: the IEP team members know the student; they were the members on the team that evaluated the student (non-discriminatory evaluation); prepared the student's educational program (IEP and appropriate education); and made the student's placement decision (least restrictive environment/placement). Thus, they are the ones best qualified to determine "manifestation." Not all IEP team members, however, may be qualified to determine "manifestation" so they need not be on the manifestation-determination team. By contrast, other LEA staff may be qualified to do so, and the LEA can add them to the team as its representatives. Apparently, the parent may not prevent these individuals from representing the LEA on the team.

Determination Standard–"Caused By" and "Direct Result":
IDEA directs the team to find that the behavior is a manifestation of the student's disability:

1. if the conduct in question was caused by, or had a direct and substantial relationship to, the child's disability; or

2. if the conduct in question was the direct result of the local educational agency's failure to implement the IEP. Section 1415(k)(1)(E)

If either (1) or (2) is true, then the behavior is a manifestation of the student's disability. If neither is true, then the behavior is not a manifestation.

◆ *Significance of "Caused By" and "Direct Result"*
The team still must consider specific evidence that may or may not point to manifestation (and, presumably, to any "unique circumstances"). However, the 2004 amendments have removed two defenses that were available to the student under the 1997 amendments of IDEA.

The first was that the child's disability impaired the ability of the child to understand the impact and consequences of the behavior (cognitive impairment). The second was that the disability impaired the child's ability to control the behavior (behavioral impairment).

With these two provisions no longer in the law, IDEA now contains more stringent requirements and imposes more accountability on the student. The manifestation team may now find that "manifestation" exists only if the behavior was "caused by" the disability or if the behavior was the "direct result" of the LEA's "failure." Before, the team needed to find only that there was a simple "manifestation of" or "relationship" between behavior and disability and that the services were not provided "consistent with" the IEP.

Determination Result–No Manifestation: Under Section 1415(k)(1)(B) through (D), a student with a disability whose behavior is not a manifestation of his or her disability may be disciplined just as any non-disabled student may be disciplined.

◆ *Significance of No Manifestation*

If the student's disability did not cause the behavior and the LEA did indeed implement the student's IEP, then the student is not a "disabled" student for the purpose of discipline and the LEA may apply the same discipline to that student as it applies to a non-disabled student. The difference is that the LEA may not terminate the student's education altogether (no cessation). This is an "equal treatment" approach, with the exception for no cessation.

Determination Result–LEA Duty if Manifestation: If the manifestation review team determines that the student's conduct is a manifestation of the disability, the IEP team must:

1. conduct a functional behavior assessment (FBA) and implement a behavioral intervention plan (BIP) for the student, if it has not already conducted such an assessment;

2. review and modify any existing behavioral intervention plans as needed to address the student's behavior; and

3. return the student to his/her current placement unless the student's parent and the LEA agency agree to change the student's placement as part of the modification of the student's BIP. Section 1415(k)(1)(F).

◆ *Significance of Post-Manifestation Determination Requirements*

Ever since the 1997 amendments were enacted, the LEA may not merely discipline the student but it must also take positive steps to address the student's behavior. If the student's behavior is a manifestation of his/her disability the LEA must develop or review the student's FBA and develop or modify the student's BIP. Note that these actions related to behavior are more specific than under the Address-the-Behavior rule. The requirement to address the behavior when it is not a manifestation is limited in that it does not require the development of a behavior plan. Functional assessment and behavior intervention only need to be pursued "as appropriate" in the absence of a manifestation determination.

XV. Exception for Weapons, Drugs, and Serious Bodily Injury

Consistent with the IDEA and NCLB principle that safe schools are the prerequisites for effective teaching and learning, Section 1415(k)(1)(G) provides for three exceptions to the manifestation determination and placement rules we just reviewed. These exceptions allow the LEAs to place students in "interim alternative educational settings" for a maximum of 45 school days, without any manifestation determination, if the student–

1. carries or possesses a "weapon" to or at school, on school premises, or to or at a school function,

2. knowingly possesses or uses "illegal drugs" or sells or solicits the sale of a "controlled substance" while at school, on school premises, or at a school function,

3. has inflicted "serious bodily injury" on another person while at school, on school premises, or at a school function.

◆ **Significance of the Change from 45 Days to 45 School Days** Under IDEA 1997, the time limitation was not more than 45 days; under the 2004 amendments, the time limitation is for not more than 45 school days. The regulations under the 1997 reauthorization defined "day" as meaning calendar day and "school day" as any day that students are in attendance at school for instructional purposes. 34 C.F.R. Section 300.9 (2002). Thus, the 2004 amendments appear to add additional time to the limit on a child's placement in an interim educational setting. Note that this also aligns the definition of "day" with the unchanged 10 school-day rule for short-term suspensions.

◆ **Significance of the Three Exceptions**
Safety is paramount, as it was under the 1997 amendments. IDEA defines "weapons," "illegal drugs," and "controlled substances" but not "serious bodily injury." The hearing officers and courts will have to determine its meaning on a case by case basis.

XVI. Determination of Setting, Section 1415(k)(2)

The interim alternative educational setting in subparagraphs (C) and (G) of paragraph (1) of Section 1415(k) shall be determined by the IEP Team.

XVII. Appeal of Disciplinary Placement or Manifestation Determination Finding

Section 1415(k)(3)(A) provides that a parent who disagrees with any decision regarding placement or the manifestation determination, may appeal by requesting a hearing about the matter.

In addition, it provides that an LEA that believes that maintaining the student's current placement is "substantially likely to result in injury to the child or to others" may request a hearing.

◆ Significance
The 2004 amendments give the local educational agencies the right to request a hearing in the "injury" situation. Again, safety is paramount.

Expedited Appeals: "The State or local agency shall arrange for an expedited hearing, which shall occur within 20 school days of the date the hearing is requested and shall result in a determination within 10 school days after the hearing." Section 1415(k)(4)(B).

◆ Significance
The 2004 amendments have added a timeline to the appeals process and removed the language that a SEA or LEA must arrange for an expedited hearing at the parent's request.

XVIII. No Disciplinary Stay Put Requirement

The basic stay put requirement in Section 1415(j) states that:

> Except as provided in subsection (k)(4), during the pendency of any proceedings conducted pursuant to this section, unless the state or local educational agency and the parents otherwise agree, the child shall remain in the then-current educational placement of the child.

Section 1415(k)(4) provides the exception to the rule for disciplinary placements:

> "When an appeal under paragraph (3) has been requested by either the parent or the local educational agency–the child shall remain in the interim alternative educational setting pending the decision of the hearing officer or until the expiration of the time period provided for in paragraph (1)(C), whichever occurs first, unless the parent and the State or local educational agency agree otherwise."

◆ *Significance of Stay Put Amendment*
The 2004 amendments greatly expand the exceptions to the general rule that a student remains in his present placement while a due process hearing (or court proceeding) is being conducted and while awaiting a decision from the hearing officer (or court). Prior to 2004, the only exception to the rule was for guns, drugs, and serious injury. The amended rule changes that result and applies to all parental appeals of "any decision regarding placement, or the manifestation determination under this subsection, or a local educational agency that believes that maintaining the current placement of the child is substantially likely to result in injury to the child or to others, may request a hearing." If there is a finding of no manifestation–necessary for schools to enforce a long-term suspension–the parents may appeal, but their child will remain in the interim alternate educational placement until the hearing officer determines the result of the hearing or the period of the suspension is concluded, whichever comes first. If there is a finding that the behavior was a manifestation, and the LEA appeals the student's return because of the likelihood of harm to himself or others, the student again must stay in the alternate educational setting until the hearing officer renders a decision. Thus, for the duration of any appeal of a more-than-10-day suspension, the student will remain in the interim placement if the LEA so chooses.

XIX. Burden of Proof

On an appeal from the team's determination, it appears that the appealing party must prove that the team's decision is not supported by the evidence it considered; here, the burden of proof is on the party bringing the appeal and consists of persuading the hearing officer/judge that the team's manifestation determination is clearly factually erroneous.

◆ *Significance of Change of Burden of Proof*
The 2004 amendments eliminate the burden of proof that the LEA formerly had to bear. Under the 1997 amendments, the LEA needed to demonstrate by "substantial evidence" that the current placement was likely to result in injury to the child or to others (IDEA 1997, Section 1415(k)(2)(A)). Also, the LEA was required to demonstrate to the hearing officer that "the child's behavior was not a manifestation of the child's disability." (IDEA 1997, Section 1415(k)(6)(B)(i)). Now, IDEA is silent about whether the LEA bears the burden of proof. Consistent with the usual rules of civil procedure and evidence, however, the party filing the appeal– whether the parent or the LEA–must carry the burden of proof. This is an unclear provision.

XX. Conduct of Hearing and Finding by Hearing Officer

The hearing officer must "hear and make a determination regarding an appeal." The hearing officer also may order a change in the student's placement by either (a) returning the student to the student's current placement or (b) ordering a change of placement to an appropriate alternative educational setting for not more than 45 school days if the hearing officer determines that maintaining the current placement of such child is "substantially likely to result in injury to the child or to others." Section 1415(k)(3)(B)(i)-(ii).

XXI. Preemptive Strike

Sometimes a student not yet classified into special education will claim that he or she is, in fact, a student with a disability and that the LEA may not discipline him or her except in accordance with IDEA. This is the "preemptive strike" that the student makes against an LEA: The student "strikes first" by invoking IDEA and its special protections.

Section 1415(k)(5)(A) provides that the student who has violated the code of student conduct may claim IDEA protections "if the (LEA) had knowledge...that the child was a child with a disability before the behavior that precipitated the disciplinary action occurred."

Section 1415(k)(5)(B) provides that the LEA is charged with ("deemed to have") that knowledge if

1. the student's parent has expressed concern in writing (unless the parent is illiterate or has a disability that prevents compliance with these requirements) to "supervisory or administrative personnel of the appropriate educational agency, or a teacher of the child, that the child is in need of special education and related services;"

2. the parent has requested an evaluation of the child pursuant to section 1414(a)(1)(B); or

3. the student's teacher or other LEA personnel has "expressed specific concerns about a pattern of behavior demonstrated by the child, directly to the director of special education of such agency or to other supervisory personnel of the agency."

◆ *Significance of Deeming*
These "deeming" provisions require an LEA to be careful when dealing with students who may have disabilities but who are not yet classified under IDEA. The LEA cannot escape providing them with IDEA protection in discipline and IDEA benefits if, in fact, the student is entitled to be classified into IDEA. Note, that there are now specific individuals that need to be informed by both a teacher or by the parents.

Exception to Preemptive Strike: An LEA is not "deemed" to have knowledge that the student is an IDEA student if the student's parent has not allowed the LEA to evaluate the student pursuant to Section 1414, has refused services under Part B after the LEA evaluated the student and found him/her eligible for IDEA, or if the LEA has evaluated the student and found that he/she is not "a not a child with a disability."

◆ *Significance of Parental Action*
The LEA may discipline students (who might be eligible for IDEA protection) as though they were not eligible if the students' parents do not avail themselves of either an evaluation or special education services. In other words, a parent cannot protest a change of placement because of their child's behavior if they

refused to admit their child to special education before the behaviors occurred.

◆ *Significance*

The "special knowledge or training" provision seems to disqualify attorneys but to allow others as aides to the parents.

XXII. Right to Appeal, Section 1415(g) and (i)

Any "aggrieved" party (the "losing party") may appeal from the local hearing officer to the state-level hearing officer and then to a federal or state court.

The party bringing a civil action shall have 90 days from the date of the decision of the hearing officer to bring such an action, or if the state has an explicit time limitation for bringing, that time limitation applies. Section 1415(i)(2)(B).

XXIII. Attorneys' Fees, Section 1415(i)

A court may award "reasonable" attorneys' fees to the "prevailing party," but the fees are subject to various limitations. Section 1415(i)(3).

Under the 2004 amendments, attorneys' fees may now be awarded to both a parent who is a prevailing party and to an SEA or LEA who prevails. An LEA may seek fees against the attorney of a parent who files a complaint or subsequent cause of action that is "frivolous, unreasonable, or without foundation" or who continued to litigate "after the litigation clearly became frivolous, unreasonable, or without foundation"; or against the parent or the parents' attorney if the complaint or cause of action was brought to "harass, cause unnecessary delay, or to needlessly increase the cost of litigation." Section 1415 (i)(3)(B)(i)(II) and (III).

Attorneys' fees may not be awarded if the parent rejects a reasonable offer of settlement, or for any time spent attending IEP meetings unless the meeting is convened as a result of an administrative hearing, judicial action or mediation. Section 1415(i)(3)(D)(ii). Attorneys' fees may also not be awarded for attending the mandatory resolution conference outlined in Section 1415(f)(1)(B)(i). Section 1415(i)(3)(D)(iii).

◆ *Significance*

The new amendments clearly set out IDEA's response to allegedly "frivolous lawsuits" by giving LEAs the new option to seek to recover legal fees against the parents' attorney. Otherwise the procedures and criteria for awarding attorneys' fees remain the same and continue to prevent courts from making arguably unconscionable fee awards. The fact that attorneys may not recover fees for their work in either IEPs or the resolution session implies that the preference is for these meetings to be conducted without the potentially adversarial presence of attorneys so that there is a higher likelihood of the parties reaching an amicable agreement.

Parent Participation: The Sixth of the Six Principles

I. Reviewing the Six Principles

The final principle is the Principle of Parent Participation. In fact, this principle is better known as parent and student partnership with educators. That is so because it offers parents, students, and educators the opportunity to be partners in making and carrying out decisions about the student's education. It is, then, a technique comparable to the Principle of Procedural Due Process–a technique of accountability.

But the Principle of Parent Participation goes beyond accountability to partnership and can assure that the first five principles are well and truly executed by everyone who has a stake in the student's education.

II. Parent Participation and Shared Decision-Making

Because we discussed many of the parent-participation provisions under the other IDEA principles, we will only briefly review them here.

One of the original (1975) purposes of IDEA and one of its continuing purposes is to protect children's rights and those of their parents or guardians, Section 1401(d)(1)(B). The 2004 amendments also add that one way of making the education of children with disabilities more effective is by "strengthening the role and responsibility of parents and ensuring that families of such children have meaningful opportunities to participate in the education of their children at school and at home." Section 1400(c)(5)(B).

The 2004 amendments now place increased responsibility on parents and hold them accountable for their action with respect to their child's education. Parents must now make decisions that define whether their child is admitted to special education and, if so, what the student will receive there. Accordingly, the amendments now require parents to inform themselves about IDEA and its provisions, and to be knowledgeable as co-educators and as advocates. A parent who does not have a firm grasp of the law and the options that IDEA grants will risk losing the parent and student rights that IDEA confers.

III. Definition of Parents, Section 1401(23)

Under the 2004 amendments, the definition of parent has been expanded (see our discussion under Overview, Part VII, definitions).

IV. Parents as Team Participants

IEP Team Member, Section 1414(d)(1)(B): A parent is a member of their child's IEP team.

Membership on the Manifestation Determination Team, Section 1415(k)(1)(E): Parents are given a role as a participant, with the LEA and other relevant members of the IEP team, to determine if a child's behavior was caused by or had a direct and substantial relationship to the child's disability or if the conduct in question resulted from the LEA's failure to implement the IEP.

◆ *Significance of Membership on Manifestation Determination Team*
IDEA does not specify who within an LEA must represent the LEA; that is a matter for the LEA to determine. It does, however, say

that the student's parents must be members of the team and that the LEA and parents must determine who on the student's IEP team is "relevant" for the purposes of determining manifestation. Not all IEP team members, however, may be qualified to determine "manifestation" so they need not be on the manifestation-determination team. By contrast, other LEA staff may be qualified to do so, and the LEA can add them to the team as its representatives. The parents may not prevent these individuals from representing the LEA on the team.

◆ *Further Significance of Membership*
IDEA still does not provide whether any single member of the team may veto decisions made by other team members. Thus, it seems that no parent may veto a "no manifestation" determination or "manifestation" determination, and neither may the LEA members over-ride a parent. IDEA still expects a consensus agreement to guide the team. If, however, any member objects to the determination, that member has recourse to the dispute-resolution provisions that we discuss in Part VI, Procedural Due Process.

Request for Hearing: Parents may request a hearing if they disagree with the placement resulting from a disciplinary action or the manifestation determination, itself. Section 1415(k)(3).

V. Parents and Private Schools, Section 1412(a)(10)(C)

We discussed the parent-choice rule under the Principle of Zero Reject.

VI. Parental Consent

We discussed parent consent, refusal to consent, and absence of consent under Non-Discriminatory Evaluation and Procedural Due Process.

VII. Parental Requests

A parent may initiate a request for an initial evaluation to determine if the child is a child with a disability. Section 1414(a)(1)(B).

A parent may now invite an individual from the services provided under Part C to attend an IEP to ensure a successful transition. Section 1414(d)(1)(D).

VIII. Parental Agreement

There also are several new provisions outlining situations where the parent and the LEA must agree before taking action.

Parents and the LEA may agree that a reevaluation may occur more frequently than once a year, or waive the requirement of an evaluation at the three-year mark. Section 1414(a)(2)(B).

Parents and the LEA may agree that an IEP team member may be excused from an IEP meeting if the member's area of the curriculum or related service is not going to be modified or discussed at the meeting. Section 1414(d)(1)(C)(i). The parents' consent must be in writing. Section 1414(d)(1)(C)(iii).

◆ *Significance*

An IEP meeting is one of the few opportunities that all of the individuals involved in a child's education come together for an in-person discussion. This "waiver" system proposes that parents will be able to forecast, before a meeting, what areas will be discussed and which areas will not be discussed. Plus, just because an area is not normally discussed (what comes to mind is regular education) that person is there to provide information towards positive behavior supports and potential integration into the general education curriculum.

Parents and the LEA may agree to make changes to an existing IEP without convening an IEP team meeting. Instead, the parents and the LEA can develop a written document to amend or modify the IEP. Section 1414(d)(3)(D).

Parents and the LEA may agree to use alternate means of meeting participation such as video conferences and conference calls. Section 1414(f).

IX. Parental Rights to Notice–General and Procedural

Parents' rights to two different kinds of notice (the general and the procedural safeguards notice) are set out under our discussion of the Principle of Due Process.

X. Parental Rights to Records

Students' records are held confidential (not accessible except on a need-to-know basis) but are accessible to parents and educators who need them in order to provide a free appropriate public education to the students.

Confidentiality of student records includes "any personally identifiable data, information, and records collected or maintained by the State and local educational agencies..." must be assured by the SEA and LEA. Section 1417(c) and Section 1412(a)(8).

Parents, however, have access, so the SEA and LEA must have a procedure which includes "an opportunity for the parents of a child with a disability to examine all records relating to such child...", Section 1415(b)(1). The SEA and LEA are both subject to the Family Educational Rights and Privacy Act (FERPA), which is codified at 20 U.S.C. Section 1232g, with regulations at 34 C.F.R., Part 99.1

FERPA requires the SEAs and LEAs to give parents, guardians and some pupils access to their own student records. If the parents wish to challenge the contents of the records, they must be given an opportunity for a hearing. FERPA also relates to confidentiality as certain parts of the record may not be released without parental consent.

XI. Parental Rights to Due Process and Mediation

We discussed these parental rights under Procedural Due Process.

XII. "Family Systems" Approach Throughout IDEA

Some related services are available directly to families, such as psychological, social work, and counseling services.

For children ages 3 through 5, additional services may be incorporated into the individualized family service plan (IFSP) (see "appropriate education," above).

◆ *Significance*
The "family systems" approach follows the theory that whatever benefits the child will benefit the child's family (and vice-versa).

Conclusion

The 2004 amendments answer many questions but also leave some unanswered. Perhaps the Department of Education Regulations will answer some; they probably will not answer all. That is where the courts have a role. Our hope is that the new IDEA will indeed improve the students' education, enhance parents' and educators' partnerships, and not become another statute that spawns litigation. And our hope also is that this booklet will aid you, the reader, in understanding IDEA, its purposes and provisions, and its significance.